Microsoft
FrontPage
2002

SIMPLY VISUAL

Microsoft® FrontPage 2002
SIMPLY VISUAL™

Perspection, Inc.

SYBEX®

San Francisco ◆ Paris ◆ Düsseldorf ◆ Soest ◆ London

Associate Publisher: Cheryl Applewood
Contracts and Licensing Manager: Kristine O'Callaghan
Acquisitions & Development Editor: Bonnie Bills
Managing Editor: Steve Johnson
Author: Bill Kunkel
Editor: Becky Dille
Production Editor: Marian Hartsough
Technical Editors: Kristy Thielen and Tracy Teyler
Book Designer: Maureen Forys, Happenstance Type-O-Rama
Electronic Publishing Specialist: Marian Hartsough
Proofreader: Shirley Todd
Indexer: Michael Brackney
Cover Designer: Daniel Ziegler
Cover Illustrator: Ziegler Design

Library of Congress Card Number: 2001090114

ISBN: 0-7821-4007-6

Manufactured in the United States of America

10 9 8 7 6 5 4 3 2 1

··

*To our spouses
who held us together and
our children who missed us
during the lengthy process.*

Perspection

Perspection, Inc., is a software training company committed to providing information and training to help people use software more effectively in order to communicate, make decisions, and solve problems. Perspection writes and produces software training books, and develops multimedia and Web-based training. This incorporates Perspection's training expertise to ensure that you'll receive the maximum return on your time. With this straightforward, easy-to-read reference tool, you get the information you need to get the job done.

We invite you to visit the Perspection Web site at:

www.perspection.com

Acknowledgments

The task of creating any book requires the talents of many hardworking people pulling together to meet almost impossible demands. For their effort and commitment, we'd like to thank the outstanding team responsible for making this book possible: the writer, Bill Kunkel; the editor, Becky Dille; the technical editors, Kristy Thielen and Tracy Teyler; the production editor, Marian Hartsough; the proofreader, Shirley Todd; and the indexer, Michael Brackney.

At Sybex, we'd like to thank Jordan Gold and Cheryl Applewood for the opportunity to undertake this project, Bonnie Bills for her editorial support, and Amy Changar, Judith Hibbard, and Cheryl Hauser for their direction and guidance with the printing process.

Perspection

Contents

Introduction   *xiii*

Chapter 1   **Creating a Web Site**   **1**

Planning a Web Site   2

Starting FrontPage   3

Using a Template   5

Adding Pages to Your Web Site   12

Opening a Web Page or Web Site   14

Moving Web Pages   16

Working with Folders View   18

Working with Hyperlinks View   19

Verifying Hyperlinks   19

Working with Navigation View   21

Applying a Theme to a Web Page   22

Working with Tasks   24

Getting Help   25

Exiting FrontPage   27

Chapter 2   **Managing and Linking Web Pages**   **29**

Opening Web Pages from Within a Web   30

Navigating Web Pages   32

Displaying Web Pages in the HTML Format   34

Previewing Web Pages   36

Creating Bookmarks   38

Linking to External Web Pages and E-Mail Addresses   40

Previewing and Printing Web Pages   42

Saving Web Pages   44

Importing Web Content   45

Exporting Web Content   47

Chapter 3   **Working with Web Page Text**   **49**

Entering Text in a Page   50

Selecting Text in a Page   51

Moving and Copying Text   52

Working with the Office Clipboard   55

Creating Bulleted and Numbered Lists   56

Finding and Replacing Text   58

Formatting Text   61

Setting Text Alignment and Spacing   63

Creating Headings and Subheadings   66

Adding Horizontal Lines   68

Checking Spelling   70

Finding the Right Words   73

Applying XML Formatting   73

Inserting WordArt Text   74

Inserting Text with Handwriting   76

Chapter 4   **Working with Web Page Graphics**   **79**

Understanding Graphics   80

Inserting Graphics   81

Cropping and Resizing Graphics   86

Copying and Pasting Graphics   88

Applying Special Effects to Graphics   89

Changing Graphic Properties   97

Changing the Way Graphics are Displayed   100

Adding Hyperlinks to Graphics   102

Working with Graphic Hotspots   105

Chapter 5   **Formatting Web Pages with Tables**   **109**

Creating Tables   110

Entering Text in a Table   113

Adding Color to a Table   115

Formatting a Table   116

Converting Text to a Table 118

Adding Cells, Rows, or Columns to Tables 119

Splitting and Merging Cells 120

Creating Table Captions 122

Deleting Table Elements 124

Filling a Table with Information 125

Adding Images to Tables 125

Changing Table Properties 127

Changing Cell Properties 129

Chapter 6   Creating Frames and Borders   133

Creating Frames Pages 134

Customizing an Existing Frames Page Template 139

Adding an Inline Frame 141

Editing an Inline Frame 143

Saving a Frameset 145

Splitting Frames 147

Deleting a Frame 148

Editing Frames Pages 149

Working with Shared Borders 153

Chapter 7   Inserting Multimedia and Special Effects   155

Changing Background Colors 156

Inserting Background Pictures 160

Adding Special Effects to Text 161

Changing the Color to Links 163

Creating a Photo Gallery 164

Adding Background Sound 168

Adding Sound Effects Using Hover Buttons 170

Inserting Video Clips 171

Creating Marquees 173

Inserting a Dynamic HTML Effect 176

Chapter 8   Drawing and Modifying Objects   179

Drawing Objects   180

Drawing Lines and Arrows   180

Drawing AutoShapes   182

Inserting AutoShapes from the Clip Gallery   184

Moving and Resizing an Object   185

Rotating and Flipping an Object   187

Choosing Object Colors   188

Adding Object Shadows   190

Creating a 3-D Object   191

Aligning and Distributing Objects   191

Arranging and Grouping Objects   193

Chapter 9   Adding Functionality to Web Pages   195

Annotating Web Pages with Comments   196

Inserting Hit Counters   197

Working with Page Banners   199

Inserting Scheduled Images   201

Inserting Timestamps   202

Inserting a Table of Contents   203

Inserting Navigation Bars   209

Creating Discussion Groups   213

Chapter 10   Gathering User Input Using Forms   217

Understanding Form Fields   218

Creating Forms   219

Inserting Text Boxes   222

Inserting Check Boxes   224

Adding Option Buttons   225

Activating a Label   226

Inserting Drop-Down Menus   227

Inserting Push Buttons   228

Contents

Inserting Pictures		230
Formatting Form Fields		231
Setting Rules for Entering Data		232
Connecting a Form to a Database		233
Saving Form Results		235
Creating a Custom Form Handler		240
Creating and Attaching a Confirmation Page		241
Chapter 11	**Publishing and Managing a Web Site**	**243**
	Publishing a Web Site	244
	Updating a Web Site	247
	Checking Web Settings	248
	Viewing Reports for a Web Site	249
	Creating and Assigning Tasks	252
Glossary		**257**
Index		*261*

Introduction

This book offers a simple visual approach to learning Microsoft FrontPage 2002. Designed for the beginner who may find the complexity of the FrontPage program intimidating, *Microsoft FrontPage 2002 Simply Visual* uses a highly visual, step-by-step format to present the fundamental tasks that any new user needs in order to get "up and running" as quickly as possible on the FrontPage program that is the industry standard.

How This Book Is Organized

Microsoft FrontPage 2002 Simply Visual is designed to be an easy-to-read and easy-to-use reference tool that helps you get your work done quickly and efficiently in a straightforward way. Each chapter is organized by tasks. Each task gives you information that is essential to performing the task. For each operation, you'll see what commands to enter and which options to select.

This book contains eleven chapters. You'll learn the essentials for creating, enhancing, publishing, and managing Web sites with the FrontPage 2002. Chapter 1 covers tasks for creating a Web site. Chapter 2 covers tasks for managing and linking Web pages. Chapter 3 and 4 cover tasks for working with Web page text and graphics. Chapter 5 covers tasks for formatting Web pages with tables. Chapter 6 covers tasks for creating frames and borders. Chapter 7 covers tasks for inserting multimedia and special effects. Chapter 8 covers tasks for drawing and modifying objects. Chapter 9 covers tasks for adding functionality to Web pages. Chapter 10 covers tasks for gathering user input using forms. Chapter 11 covers tasks for publishing and managing a Web site.

How to Make Good Use of This Book

We recommend using this book as a kind of beginner's reference. Use the index or table of contents to find the command or feature you want to learn about and go directly there. Each basic operation is presented as a step-by-step procedure, with illustrations to guide you. Simple but realistic examples allow you to try out most procedures on your own. As key terms are introduced, you'll find capsule definitions in the margin. (These definitions are also gathered into a Glossary at the end of the book, so you can look up a term at any time.) Margin notes also provide alternative methods to accomplish particular steps and summarize important concepts.

Every reader should begin with the first chapter, especially if you are not at all familiar with FrontPage 2002. After that, you can jump to any of the chapters that meet your needs. Keep the book near your workstation for quick access as you work on your projects. If a command or procedure confuses you, you can easily flip to the two or three pages that describe it.

We hope this book serves you as a useful guide as you learn and use FrontPage 2002.

1 Creating a Web Site

FrontPage 2002 is a program that empowers even the most inexperienced computer user with the tools to create and launch a **Web site** or **Web page**. From the planning stages through the development process, this chapter is designed to familiarize you with the terminology and overall operation of FrontPage. Subsequent chapters discuss the specifics of site management and the details of web design and execution.

This chapter takes you through the planning stages, gets you up and running on the program, discusses the virtues and limitations of templates, and summarizes the various views. You are introduced to hyperlinks, HTML, Wizards, Mother page, Child page, Parent page, and the other commonly encountered features of designing a Web site using FrontPage. You will also learn about more aesthetic design considerations, such as the use of themes in site development.

Planning a Web Site

Before you begin developing your Web site in FrontPage, there are several issues to consider and a few decisions to make. First, of course, is the question of what type of **Web page** or **Web site** you want to build. What is the focus of your design? Are you looking to create a personal page or site? Maybe you want to create a business site. Perhaps you're a hobbyist, anxious to display your extensive knowledge and imagery on your favorite subject, or a collector who wants to show off your best pieces in a personal, online museum.

> **TIP** FrontPage 2002 uses "web" to mean Web site.

After you've decided the kind of Web page or Web site you want to produce, you should consider the question of content. Stagnant sites will not draw repeat visitors, and if you want to generate traffic, you will have to update the material on a regular basis. Do you intend to generate all this content on your own, or will you be recruiting other people to produce the content? Content creation is usually the most overlooked aspect of Web design, but unless your ambition is limited to producing something such as an online family log, with photos of family and pets, birthdates, and a list of everyone's hobbies and interests, creating content might constitute your single greatest challenge.

Attracting and growing a vibrant base of visitors to your **Web site** or **Web page** requires you to have a good idea of who will make up your audience. You need to consider issues of demographics—who is interested in your Web site, how old are they, and so on. Are you aiming at surfers with a casual interest in your subject matter, or are you focusing on the expert audience?

After you've dealt with these important matters, you need to decide whether you intend to work from a **template** or create your site from scratch. All but the most experienced users should begin with one of the templates provided with FrontPage. These templates offer a satisfying variety of formats representing the most popular Web site styles. You can also customize a template to your specific needs by replacing the headers, textual arrangements, or graphic elements.

After you've familiarized yourself with the basics of Web site creation and maintenance, you can become more adventurous.

Web site

A single page or collection of pages about a given topic or topics organized and published on the World Wide Web.

Web page

A single document on the World Wide Web with its own unique URL (Uniform Resource Locator). Web sites generally contain several, linked Web pages.

Template

A pre-formatted Web page or site.

Starting FrontPage

When you first open FrontPage, the program window opens, displaying windows, menus, and a task bar. The Title bar across the top of the screen contains the program and Web site name, with the Menu bar directly below it, and the Standard and Formatting toolbars below the Menu bar. The **Views** bar, where you select the format in which you want to work, runs vertically down the left side of the screen (the program's default is Page View), and the View tabs—which offer access to Normal, **HTML**, and Preview modes—occupy a small area at the bottom of the screen. These features will be explained in the topics below.

Start FrontPage Using the Start Menu

1. Click the **Start** button on the taskbar, point to **Programs**, and then click **Microsoft FrontPage**. The FrontPage program window opens.

Title bar Menu bar Standard toolbar Formatting toolbar

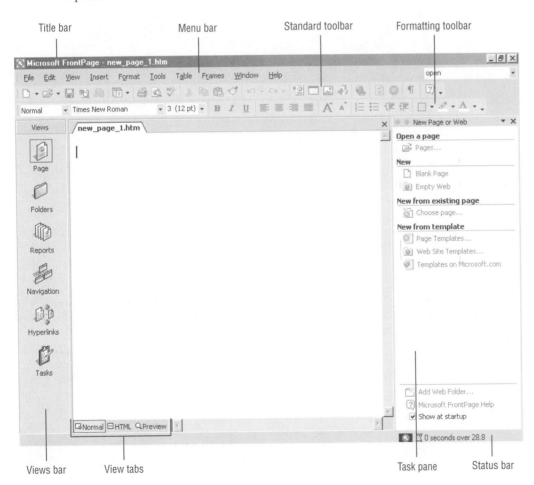

Views bar View tabs Task pane Status bar

Views
The various layouts in which you can work on your web site.

HTML
The programming language used to create Web pages and Web sites. The abbreviation stands for hypertext markup language.

> **NOTE**
> A dialog box opens the first time you start FrontPage so that you can select it as your default Web page editor. If you decline, you can choose to make FrontPage the default editor later. Choose Tools ➤ Options, click the General tab, click the Check if FrontPage is the default editor for pages check box to select it, and then click the OK button.

2. Click the **View** menu, and then click **Task Pane** (Choose **View** ➤ **Task Pane**), if necessary. The New Page Or Web task pane opens.

> **NOTE**
> When you perform certain actions, such as inserting a new blank page, the New Page or Web task pane closes to provide more room for the central display window where the page opens. To restore the task pane, choose View ➤ Toolbars ➤ Task Pane.

> **WARNING**
> Before you begin work on a new site, close the blank page that opens when you start FrontPage 2002 or it will be added as the first page of your site automatically.

Using a Template

The Web site templates displayed on the New Page or Web task pane include ten Web site wizards. A **wizard** is a series of pre-configured sequential dialog boxes that guide you step-by-step through complicated processes. The Web site template wizards include One Page Web, Corporate Presence, Customer Support, Database Interface, Discussion Web, Empty Web, Import Web, SharePoint-based Team Web Site, Personal Web, and Project Web.

Wizard
A series of dialog boxes that leads you through a task.

Create a Web Site Using a Template

1. Choose **View ➤ Task Pane**, if necessary. The New Page or Web task pane opens.

2. In the **New WebPage or Web** task pane, click **Web Site Templates**. The Web Site Templates dialog box opens.

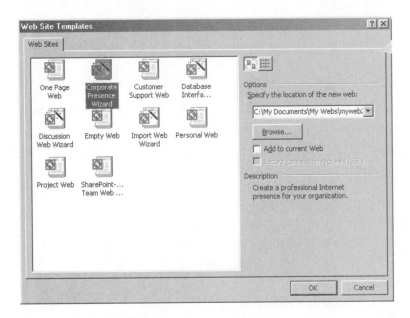

3. Click a wizard icon, and then click the **OK** button. Each wizard takes you through different steps.

NOTE For this example, the Corporate Presence Wizard is selected. The first Corporate Presence Web Wizard dialog box opens (all subsequent dialog boxes in this wizard carry the same name), explaining that the wizard is about to ask you a series of questions that will define the parameters of your site. For the purpose of illustrating all the features of this Wizard, all check boxes are selected in each Wizard dialog box.

4. Click the **Next** button to continue.

5. The next Wizard dialog box opens, offering six categories of site pages that can appear in a web. The **Home** option is already selected, as this is required for every web site. Other options include **What's New**, **Products/Services**, **Table Of Contents**, **Feedback Form**, and **Search Form**. Click the check boxes to select or clear the options you want. Click the **Next** button to continue.

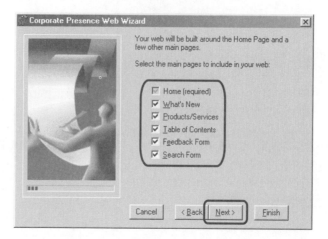

6. The next Wizard dialog box opens, offering a series of features that you might want to include on the home page: **Introduction**, **Mission Statement**, **Company Profile**, and **Contact Information**. Click the check boxes to select or clear the options you want. Click the **Next** button to continue.

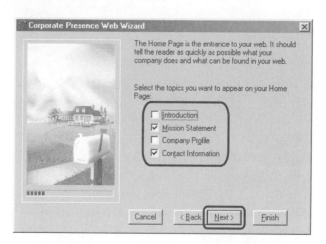

7. The next Wizard dialog box opens, containing potential components of the What's New Page. The components include **Web Changes** (site updates), **Press Releases**, and **Articles And Reviews** (archives). Click the check boxes to select or clear the options you want. Click the **Next** button to continue.

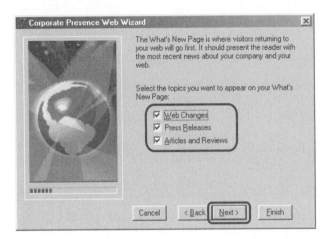

8. The next Wizard dialog box opens, containing links to Web pages with information about all the products and services your corporation offers. You place numbers in each of the two boxes representing the number of **Products** and **Services** that your company offers. Click the check boxes to select or clear the options you want. Click the **Next** button to continue.

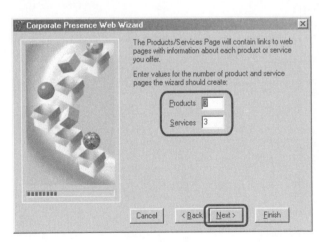

9. The next Wizard dialog box opens, containing three additional items that can be used to supplement each Product and Service page. The three extra product features are:

◇ **Product image**—A picture of the product.

◇ **Pricing information**—A brief description of the product pricing.

◇ **Information request form**—A form users can fill out and submit to request additional information about the product.

The three extra service features are:

◇ **Capabilities list**—What will the service provide the customer.

◇ **Reference accounts**—Who else has used the service that the customer might know.

◇ **Information request form**—A form users can fill out and submit to request additional information about the service.

Click the check boxes to select or clear the options you want. Click the **Next** button to continue.

10. The next Wizard dialog box opens, displaying a Feedback Form, which provides a list of information you might want to collect from site visitors. This includes **Full Name**, **Job Title**, **Company Affiliation**, **Mailing Address**, **Telephone Number**, **FAX Number**, and **E-Mail Address**. Click the check boxes to select or clear the options you want. Click the **Next** button to continue.

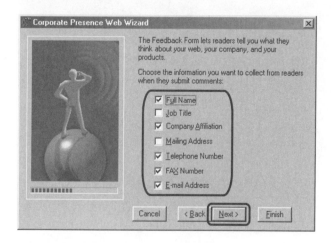

11. The next Wizard dialog box opens, displaying additional Feedback From options. It stores e-mail from visitors to your site. This box asks whether you want to use the standardized tab-delimited format to make the information compatible with database and spreadsheet programs. Click the check boxes to select or clear the options you want. Click the **Next** button to continue.

12. The next Wizard dialog box opens, containing three presentation options for your Table of Contents page: **Keep Page List Up-To-Date Automatically**; **Show Pages Not Linked Into Web**; and **Use Bullets For Top-Level Pages**. To display a set of links to every page in your web, similar to the Hyperlink view in FrontPage, select all. Click the **Next** button to continue.

13. The next Wizard dialog box opens, containing a list of the information you can include on the top and bottom of each page. Options for the top include **Your Company Logo**, **Page Title**, and **Links To Your Main Web Pages**. Options for the bottom include **Links To Your Main Web Pages**, **E-Mail Address Of Your Webmaster**, **Copyright Notice**, and **Date Page Was Last Modified**. Click the check boxes to select or clear the options you want. Click the **Next** button to continue.

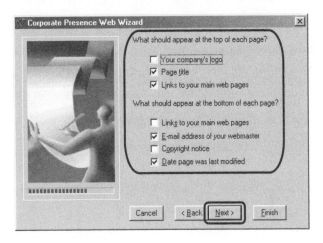

14. The next Wizard dialog box opens, offering an option of generating an "Under Construction" icon to represent a page that is not yet finished. Select an option button, and then click the **Next** button to continue.

15. The next Wizard dialog box opens, requesting your company's full name and its commonly-used name, as well as its street address. Enter or edit the information, and then click the **Next** button to continue.

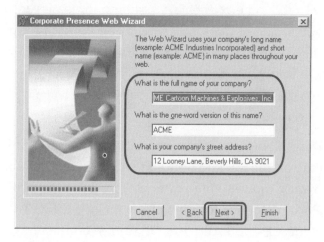

16. The next Wizard dialog box opens, requesting your company's phone, fax, and e-mail contact information. Enter or edit the information, and then click the **Next** button to continue.

17. The next Wizard dialog box opens, offering you the option of introducing a theme into your site. To select a theme, click the **Choose Web Theme** button. In the Choose Theme dialog box, select a theme, and then click the **OK** button. Click the **Next** button to continue.

18. The final Wizard dialog box opens, informing you that the questions are finished and offering you the option to show Tasks view after the web is uploaded. Click the **Show Tasks View After The Web Is Uploaded** check box to select it, and then click the **Finish** button. The Web site opens in Task view.

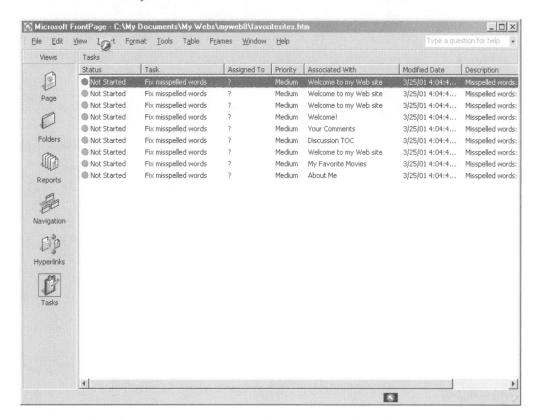

NOTE In Tasks view, the status and priority of each page is displayed. You can work on any of the pages by right clicking them and selecting either Start Task or Edit Task from the shortcut menu.

NOTE With FrontPage, you can create a Web site for compatibility with specific browsers. For example, you can create a Web site for compatibility with both Microsoft Internet Explorer and Netscape Navigator, or for compatibility with all version 4.0 browsers. If you choose specific compatibility options, menu commands that are not supported will be gray out (not available) as you create the Web site.

Adding Pages to Your Web Site

Hyperlinks
Links on your Web page that take you to another location in cyberspace.

Whether you have the basic Web site created via a wizard, or are beginning from scratch, you will eventually need to add new pages to the site. New pages can be blank or template based, so it is also possible to integrate template pages with your own pages that you created from scratch. After you create the new page, you need to create **hyperlink** to the existing Web. The task pane contains an extensive selection of single-page templates.

Add Pages to a Web Site

1. To add a new page, in Folders view, right-click in the blank area of the Folders window, point to **New**, and then click **Page**. A new file appears in the Folder List, and is assigned a default name which is highlighted and framed in a box.

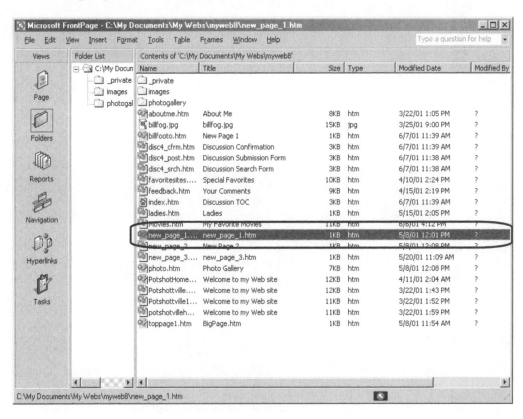

2. To rename the page, click the name to select it, type your new name, and then click the file name icon at the beginning of the line.

3. To link your page to the existing web, in the Folders view, drag the file name icon to the **Navigation** button on the Views bar. When the Navigation view opens, drag the file name icon into the Navigation view. Expanding and contracting perforated lines appear any place where your page can be positioned.

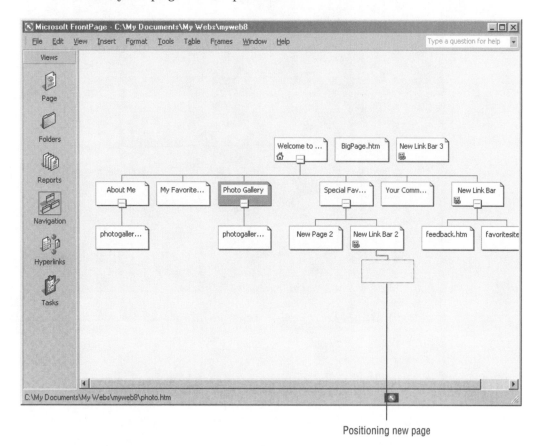

Positioning new page

To delete a page from your web, click the page you want to delete in Navigation view, and then press the Delete key. You can determine whether you want the page deleted from your hard drive or just from the web.

4. When the new page is where you want it, release the mouse button to position the page.

When adding new pages to your web, remember to include them on your web in Navigation view, or the page won't appear in the navigation buttons or links that are created by FrontPage.

5. Double-click the new page to open it for editing.

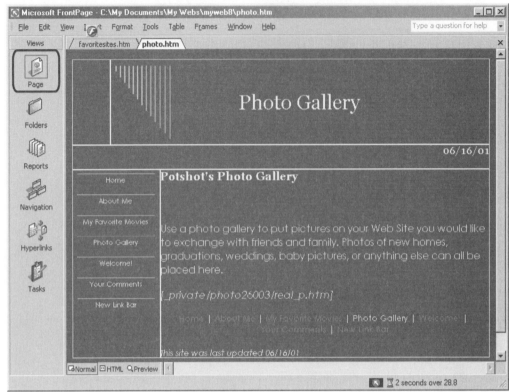

Opening a Web Page or Web Site

URL
The code signifying a location or "address" in cyberspace.

Opening a web page or web site is a simple procedure and can be accomplished using the Open button drop-down arrow on the Standard toolbar. You can open a Web page or Web site from your local hard drive, a network drive, or a Web server using an Uniform Resource Locator (**URL**).

> **NOTE** By default, FrontPage opens the last web site you worked on every time you open the program. If you open a new site while another site is still open, the new site opens in a new FrontPage window.

Open a Web Page in Page View

1. Click the **Page** button on the Views bar.

2. Choose **File ➤ Open** or click the **Open** button [image] on the Standard toolbar. The Open File dialog box opens.

3. Click the **Look In** drop-down arrow [image], and then select the folder location of the Web page you want to open.

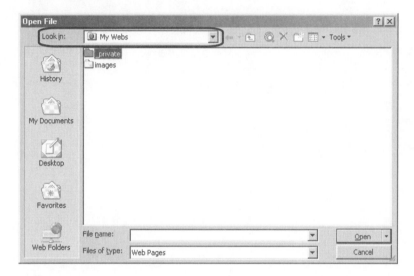

4. Select the page you want to open from the page list in the working folder or type the URL of the page you want to open in the **File Name** box.

5. Click the **Open** button. The Web page opens.

Open a Web Site

1. Choose **File ➤ Open Web** or click the **Open** button drop-down arrow [image] on the Standard toolbar, and then click **Open Web**. The Open Web dialog box opens.

2. Click the **Look In** drop-down arrow ![arrow], and then select the folder location (hard drive-based or network-based) containing the Web site you want to open.

3. Select the Web site you want to open or type the URL of the site you want to open in the **Web Name** box.

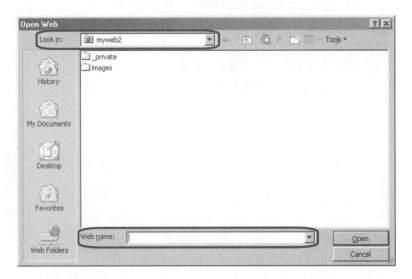

4. Click the **Open** button. The Web site opens. Webs in the Folder List can then be accessed by double-clicking them.

> **TIP** If you've recently accessed a Web site or Web page, you can use the File menu to quickly open it again. Choose File ➢ Recent Webs or Recent Files, and then click the web or file you want.

Moving Web Pages

After you've created and saved a new page, you can move to it to different location in your web by simply dragging the page in Navigation view.

Move a Web Page

1. Click the **Navigation** button on the Views bar. The existing site now opens in its branching, hierarchical view in the main window. Between the Views bar and the main window, a Folder List opens.

2. To move a new page into your site, click the page in the Folder List, and then drag it to the position you want it to occupy on your site.

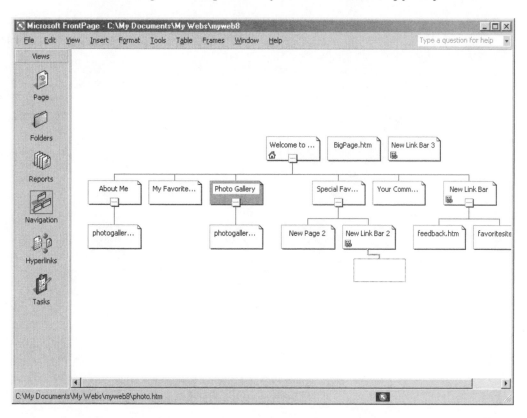

Working with Folders View

The Folders view displays all files and folders currently under construction. To access this view, click the Folders button on the Views bar. Three folders (Web, Private, and Images) are created for all new template-based sites, regardless of the Wizard you used.

Folders under construction

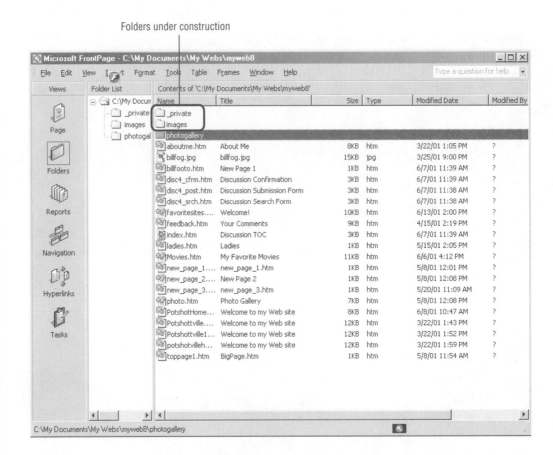

The Web folder is tagged by the web's location, the name that you entered in to Specify The Location Of The New Web box. If you did not specify a location, your web is stored in the default location C://MyDocuments/MyWebs/directory. The Private folder contains any information obtained from special forms or any other data input objects on the site and cannot be accessed by a visitor. Finally, the Images folder enables you to store any images, from digital photos to clip art, which are part of this web.

You can open files in this view by double-clicking them. Files will be opened in Page view. You can delete files from your web in Folders view by selecting the file and pressing the Delete key.

Working with Hyperlinks View

The Hyperlinks view offers a simplified presentation of the source and destination of internal and external hyperlinks that appear on a given page. These links are displayed in a flowchart fashion.

Display Hyperlinks View

1. Select the page you want to display from either the Folders or Navigation views.

2. Click the **Hyperlinks** button on the Views bar. The page, with its hyperlinks, opens.

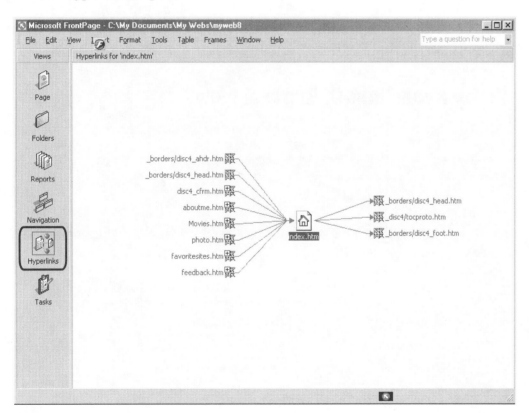

Verifying Hyperlinks

When you have a layout of your hyperlinks, you'll want to confirm that they're accurately linked. Because sites are purchased, re-started, and even shut down on a regular basis, URLs to external links can change. You can confirm the accuracy of your hyperlinks by using the Hyperlinks View to display links and their contents.

Clicking the "+" box for any page displays that page's links. This provides a quick, easy method to expand or shrink the link view to display the entire link structure of the pages, or only those that link directly to the home page.

Double-clicking a page automatically displays that page in Page view and moves it to the center of the hyperlink display when you revert to Hyperlinks view.

> **NOTE**   In Hyperlinks View, links are displayed using a variety of buttons. A page containing a globe button represents the presence of a link to the Web. A page featuring a picture button signifies a link to a visual element, and an envelope button indicates the hyperlink leads to a piece of e-mail.

The Hyperlinks view displays your links, but it doesn't assure that they are correct. To verify links, use the Reports view.

Verify Hyperlinks in Reports View

1. Click the **Reports** button on the Views bar. The Reports view opens.

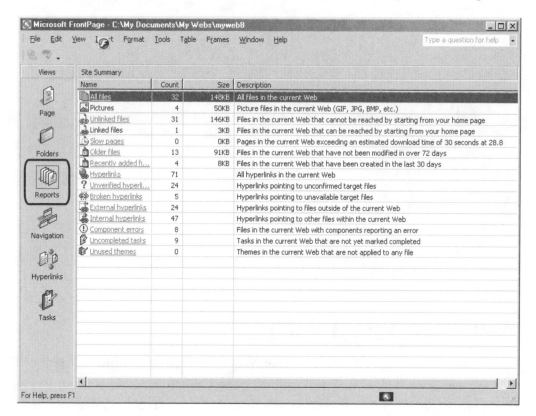

2. Click the **Verify Hyperlinks** button 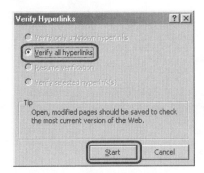 on the Reporting toolbar. The Verify Hyperlinks dialog box opens.

3. Make sure the **Verify All Hyperlinks** check box is selected, and then click the **Start** button.

4. If you aren't online at this point and any of the links are to an Internet URL, you will be prompted to connect to the World Wide Web. Front-Page 2002 automatically checks any links that haven't been confirmed as correct and generates a report. Scan the Status column and make sure you don't have any broken links. If there are none, the process is over.

> **TIP** It is often easier to work on a site when you are offline.

> **NOTE** If you do have a broken link, right-click it, and then click Edit Hyperlink on the shortcut menu. The Edit Hyperlink dialog box opens with the link of the page in question, and a blank space for you to enter the correct address. There are also two boxes so that you can choose to apply the change to all pages where the link appears, or only in selected places.

Working with Navigation View

The Navigation view structures the pages of a web in the form of a flowchart. The web is displayed in a hierarchical format, with the home page, or **Mother page**, at the top of the chart. The pages that branch off directly from the home page (**Parent page**) are considered **Child pages** of the home page.

Any page that links directly to the home page is a Child page, but it can also be a Parent page if it, in turn, produces Child pages that link to it. Each page that

Mother page
FrontPage's name for a site's original source page, the top page of the site, because all other pages in a web lead back to it.

Parent page
Any page within a web that has pages linked back to it.

Child page
Any page that links back to a Mother page or Parent page.

opens one tier below the page it is linked to is a Child page. The terms Parent and Child page are therefore relational in nature. The higher page in the hierarchy will always be the parent to any linked lower page, which will always be the child. Therefore, a second-level page can be both the Child of a page and the Parent page of a lower-level Child page.

Navigational view provides an easy way to view your pages. It also provides the easiest method for re-arranging the order of your pages, or creating new Parent pages. You can reposition a page in your web by dragging a page.

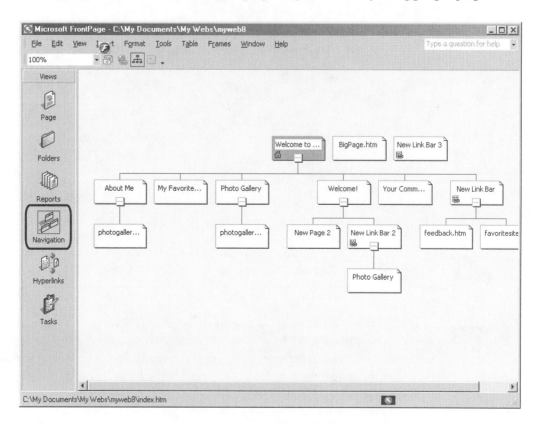

Applying a Theme to a Web Page

While the templates provide a nice structure and underpinning for your site, they can sometimes look a little generic. Using **Themes**, you can personalize your web with the use of color, banners, buttons, and bullets.

Initially, a site made from a template will probably be adequate for your needs, but as you visit more sites and become more familiar with the Internet, you will notice telltale indications of template-based sites.

Themes
Motifs that visually unify your site.

22

Themes are crucial in building an original, distinctive site. When your needs become more sophisticated, no template will suit all your needs. Using themes is the most accessible and user-friendly method to enhance your web.

Format a Web Page Using a Theme

1. Choose **Format** ➤ **Theme**. The Themes dialog box opens. The default theme is Profile.

2. Decide whether you want the theme to apply to **All Pages** or **Selected Page(s)**, and then click the corresponding option in the upper-left corner of the window.

3. Select a theme. The theme's banner, buttons, and headline styles appear in preview window.

4. Click the check boxes to select the options that enable you to further modify the theme: **Vivid Colors** (sharpens colors within the theme), **Active Graphics** (graphics with a semi-3-D quality that cause the buttons and text to "pop"), **Background Picture** (places either a shade or an image as the background), and **Apply Using Cascading Style Sheet** (CSS) (lines up all options and introduces buttons and other style-based features into the page). Experiment with these options to see the style change in the preview window.

5. Click the **Modify** button to display additional options. Click the **Colors**, **Graphics**, or **Text** buttons to modify the theme. Experiment with each of these options to see the changes reflected in the preview window.

6. When you are satisfied with your choices, click the **OK** button to apply the theme to the Web site.

Working with Tasks

Tasks are specific objectives that must be met to complete your web. Tasks can be assigned, created, or deleted.

Create New Tasks

1. Click the **Tasks** button on the Views bar. The tasks that the Corporate Presence Wizard created earlier are listed on the screen.

2. Choose **File ➢ New ➢ Task**. The New Task dialog box opens.

3. In the **Task Name** box, enter the name of the task.

4. In the **Assigned To** box, enter a name or click the drop-down arrow ▾, and then select a name.

5. In the **Description** box, type a description of the task.

6. Click the **Low**, **Medium**, or **High** option button to set the Priority level.

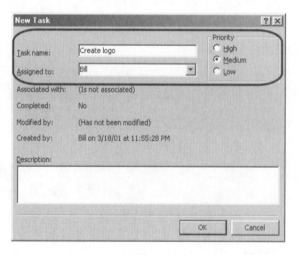

7. Click the **OK** button. The task appears in the Tasks view.

8. In Tasks view, right-click a task, and then click **Start Task**.

> **NOTE** This is the same that you would do when beginning completion of any existing task currently listed as Not Started.

9. When you have completed working on the task, click the **Save** button 🖫 on the Standard toolbar.

10. Click the **Yes** button or the **No** button to mark the task as complete or incomplete. If it's complete, click the **Yes** button. You are informed of the date when this file was last saved and asked if you want to save the most recent work on the task. If you click the **No** button, the process is ended and you can no longer change the status of the task.

11. Click the **Tasks** button on the Views bar. The circle in front of the task should now be green.

> **TIP**
> When you open, close, and reopen FrontPage, and then click Task View, the completed tasks no longer appear. However, if you right-click Tasks on the Task bar, you can access the Show History command, which maintains a list of all completed tasks.

Getting Help

FrontPage provides an extensive Help system to guide you in completing tasks. Whenever you encounter a problem, choose the Help menu. Numerous options are available to you, including Microsoft FrontPage Help. Clicking Help activates your **Office Assistant**, an animated Help feature in the form of a cartoon paperclip named Clippit. The Assistant produces a dialog balloon, so that you can ask your question, then click either the Search button or the Options button. The appearance of the dialog box that accompanies the Office Assistant changes over time. It will always reflect the last topic that you accessed by default.

Office Assistant
An animated Help feature that displays helpful tips while you are working in FrontPage.

> **NOTE**
> Click the Options button in the Office Assistant to open a dialog box that includes the Gallery tab, where you can select a different Office Assistant, and the Options tab, which includes a list of features that can be toggled on or off by clicking the boxes next to the features.

> **NOTE**
> If you want to know more about any command or button in FrontPage, point to it with your mouse and pause; additional information will pop-up in the form of a ScreenTip.

Use the Help Menu

1. Choose **Help** ➤ **Microsoft FrontPage Help**.

TIP You can also access Help at any time by pressing F1.

2. When the Office Assistant appears, type your question in the text box, and then click the **Search** button.

NOTE Click the Search button to generate a list of subjects related to the information you are seeking. Click the subjects to link to information on the topic under discussion.

Use the Ask A Question Box

1. On the Title bar, click in the **Ask a Question** box.

2. Type your question.

3. Press the Enter key to display A list of help topics related to your question.

4. Click a topic to view it.

Show or Hide the Office Assistant

1. Choose **Help** ➢ **Show The Office Assistant**. The Office Assistant is turned on.

2. To turn off the Office Assistant, choose **Help** ➢ **Hide The Office Assistant**, or right-click the **Office Assistant**, and then click **Hide**.

TIP   The Office Assistant provides interactive help. If you see a Show Me link in Help, click the link to display a demonstration of how to perform the task.

Exiting FrontPage

After you finish working on a web, you can close it and open another one, or close it and quit FrontPage. Closing a web makes more computer memory available for other processes. Closing a web is different from quitting

FrontPage: after you close a web, FrontPage is still running. When you're finished using FrontPage, you can quit the program. To protect your files, always quit FrontPage before turning off your computer.

Close a Web

1. Choose **File** ➢ **Close Web**.

If you have made any changes to the web since last saving it, the Office Assistant asks if you want to save the web.

2. Click the **Yes** button to save any web changes; click the **No** button to close the web without saving any changes; or click the **Cancel** button to return to the web without closing it.

Quit FrontPage

1. Choose **File** ➢ **Exit**, or click the **Close** button ☒ on the FrontPage program window title bar.

NOTE   When you close a file that you've modified but have not yet saved, a dialog box opens asking if you want to save your changes.

2. Click the **Yes** button to save any web changes, or click the **No** button to ignore any changes.

2 Managing and Linking Web Pages

Now that you have looked at the big picture, and you have some idea of what you can do with webs, it's time to examine the specific components that comprise the web design interface of FrontPage. You will learn to open Web pages from within a web and look at the HTML and Preview modes to create, save, and link bookmarks, pages, and webs.

Opening Web Pages from Within a Web

Multitasking

The capability to open multiple pages or documents at the same time.

FrontPage allows you to **multitask**, which means you can have more than one Web page open at the same time. After you open a Web site, you can quickly open Web pages in Folders, Navigation, or Page views instead of using the Open button on the Standard toolbar or the Open command on the File menu.

> **NOTE** Any pages you have not linked in a web will be stored as individual documents which can be opened and edited.

Open a Web Page in Folders or Navigation View

1. Open the Web site with the Web page you want to open.

2. Click the **Folders** or **Navigation** button on the Views bar.

2. Double-click the icon or file name representing the page you want to access. The Web page opens.

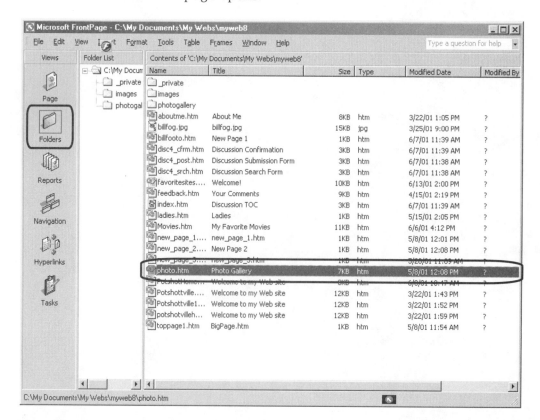

Open a Web Page Using the Folder List

1. Open the Web site with the Web page you want to open.

2. Click the **Page** button on the Views bar.

3. Click the **Toggle Pane** button 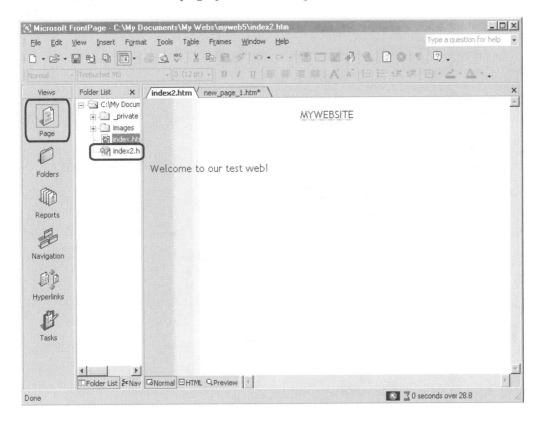 on the Standard toolbar. The Folder List opens in the Page view between the Views bar and the primary display window.

4. Double-click the page you want to open.

5. Click the **Close** button ☒ on the Folder List.

Close a Web Page

1. Choose **File** ➢ **Close**, or click the **Close** button ⊠ on the document tab bar. If you have made any changes to the Web page since last saving it, FrontPage asks if you want to save the Web page.

2. Click the **Yes** button to save any web changes; click the **No** button to close the Web page without saving any changes; or click the **Cancel** button to return to the web without closing it.

Navigating Web Pages

Navigating among Web pages can be accomplished using document tabs in the Page view or the Windows menu.

Navigate Web Pages Using Document Tabs

1. Click the **Page** button on the Views bar.

2. Click the document tab with the page you want to display.

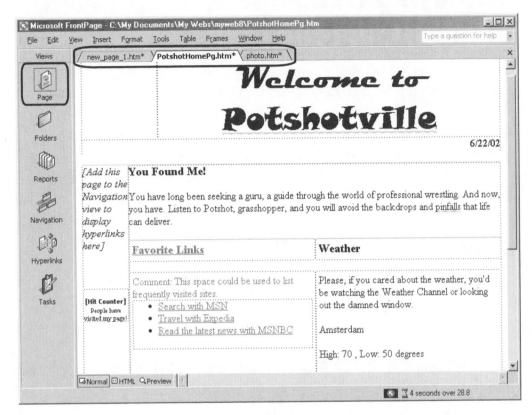

Navigate Web Pages Using the Windows Menu

1. Click the **Window** menu. This displays a list of up to nine open Web pages.

2. Click the page you want to open. The Web page opens in Page view.

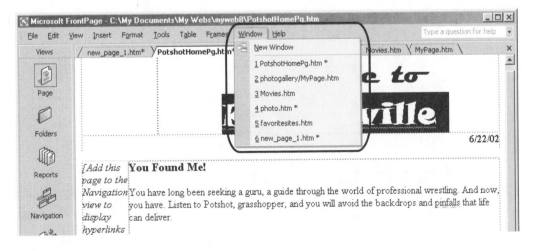

Displaying Web Pages in the HTML Format

One of the most user-friendly components of FrontPage is its capability to automatically convert text and images into HTML format. If you're familiar with HTML, you might be comfortable enough to work in this mode. HTML adds a series of format instructions to your content using tags, such as <i>, that indicate how to format the text for display on the web. FrontPage uses colored text to distinguish between various elements when working in HTML format. Your text opens in black, while all HTML tags are displayed in blue.

Display a Web Page in HTML

1. Open the Web page you want to display in the HTML format.

2. Click the **HTML** tab at the bottom of the window. The Web page appears in HTML coded form.

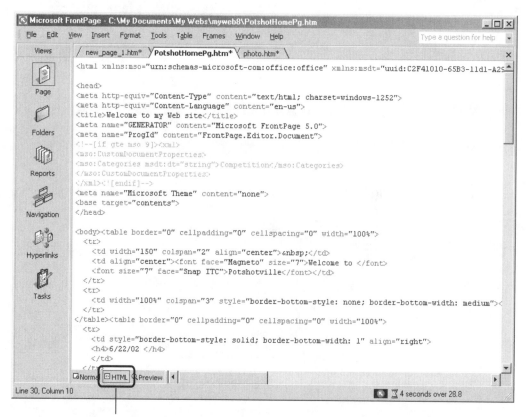

View web in HTML mode

> **NOTE** When you save a web or Web page, it is actually being saved in HTML format. And, while it might appear somewhat daunting at first glance, you can easily learn basic HTML scripting. Many Webmasters prefer the control they get by working directly in HTML.

Display HTML Tags in Normal View

1. Open the Web page you want to display HTML tags.

2. Choose **View ➢ Reveal Tags**. HTML tags appear in capsule-size, six-sided frames within the text.

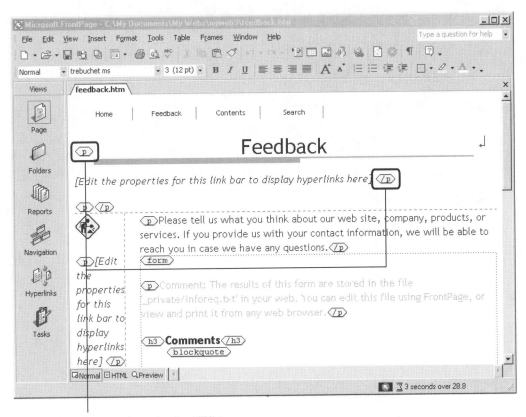

Examples of starting and ending HTML tags

Previewing Web Pages

The Preview view displays how the web will appear to a visitor who is browsing with Microsoft's Internet Explorer. Because each browser can display your site differently, you will want to examine your site using several of the most popular browser formats. If you have installed Internet Explorer on your computer, the FrontPage Preview option is enabled. When you are ready to see how your page will look to visitors, click the Preview tab. It is next to the Normal and HTML views in the central display window, above the taskbar.

Preview a Web Page Using the Preview Tab

1. Open the Web page you want to preview.

2. Click the **Preview** tab at the bottom of the window.

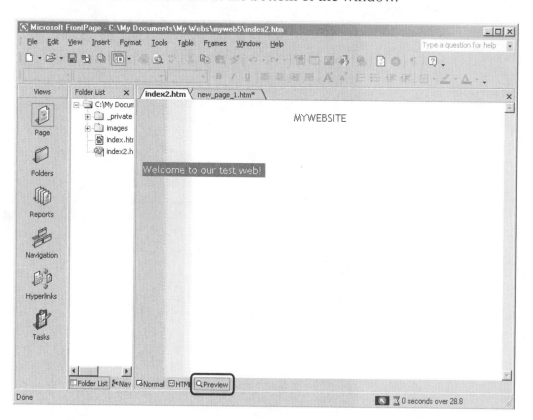

Preview a Web Page Using a Browser

1. Open the Web page you want to preview.

2. Choose **File** ➢ **Preview In Browser**. The Preview In Browser dialog box opens.

3. Click the browser you want to use to preview your site or page.

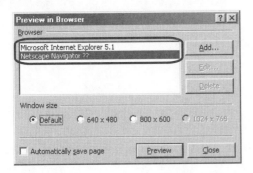

NOTE You must have previously installed the full version of other browsers like Netscape Navigator if you want to preview how your pages will appear to users of those browsers.

4. Click a Window size option button. This option determines the size of the window in which the web will be previewed. If your computer monitor's resolution is 800 x 600 or higher, click the 640 x 480 option button to get a preview of how your site will appear on a monitor with lower resolution capabilities. Otherwise, click the Default option button.

TIP To be sure that you have saved the page you want to preview, click the Automatically Save Page check box to select it in the Preview in Browser dialog box.

5. Click the **Preview** button.

Adding a Browser in FrontPage

During its installation, FrontPage automatically searches for and installs the programming required to interface with any browsers already installed on your computer.

If you want to add additional browsers in FrontPage after it is installed, open the Preview in Browser dialog box, then click the Add button. The Add Browser dialog box opens. You can then type the browser's name and the command you want to use to open it. You can also click the Browse button to access the browser directly from a Windows File dialog box. Other options on the Preview In Browser dialog box enable you to edit or delete existing browser entries.

Creating Bookmarks

When you are surfing the web, a bookmark in your browser is a shortcut to a Web site or page, a placeholder so that you can quickly access a favorite location in cyberspace. In FrontPage, the term **bookmark** is used to denote a link that helps the reader navigate a long web page quickly, rather than having to scroll through it.

Create a Bookmark

1. In Page view, select the text or graphic element within the page that you want to bookmark. If you have broken the page into sections, section headers make excellent bookmarks.

Highlight area to be bookmarked

2. Choose **Insert ➢ Bookmark**. The Bookmark dialog box opens.

3. In the **Bookmark Name** box, type a bookmark a name.

4. Click the **OK** button. You have now created a bookmark. This bookmark is visually signified in the Normal view with a perforated underline.

Once a bookmark is set, it appears with a perforated underline

NOTE You can delete bookmarks. To delete a bookmark, choose Insert ➤ Bookmark. Select the bookmark you want to delete, and then click the Clear button. When you delete a bookmark, any hyperlinks that connected to the deleted destination are *not* automatically adjusted and are now dead links that you need to locate and repair. (See the section *Verifying Hyperlinks* in Chapter 1.)

To rename a bookmark, right-click the bookmark, and then click Bookmark Properties. In the Bookmark Name box, type the new name, and then click the OK button. FrontPage does the rest, reconfiguring any relevant hyperlinks.

Navigate to Bookmarks

After you have placed one or more bookmarks, they are available to navigate to in the Bookmark dialog box.

1. Choose **Insert ➤ Bookmark**. The Bookmark dialog box opens.

2. In the **Other Bookmarks On This Page** box, click the bookmark in which you want to navigate.

3. Click the **GoTo** button.

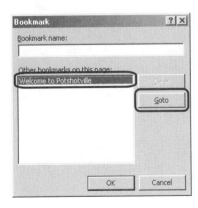

Linking to External Web Pages and E-Mail Addresses

In the first chapter, you learned how to link internal pages in your web via the Navigation view. You can also link external pages to your web from a local or Internet location. Creating a link to external pages allows users to access additional information. Linking to external sites cannot be accomplished through the Navigation view. You can also create links to e-mail addresses. Creating a link to an e-mail address allows users of your web page to contact you, or any other e-mail recipient that you specify.

Link to an External Web Page

1. Open a page of your site in Page view.

2. Select the word or words you want to link from.

3. Click the **Insert Hyperlink** button ▦ on the Standard toolbar. The Insert Hyperlink dialog box opens.

4. Click the **Existing File Or Web Page** button on the **Link To** bar. The words you entered as the link on your Web page appear in the **Text To Display** box.

5. Under **Look In**, click **Current Folder**, **Browsed Pages**, or **Recent Files** to location a file or Web page and select the one to which you want to link, or type a URL to access an Internet location in the **Address** box.

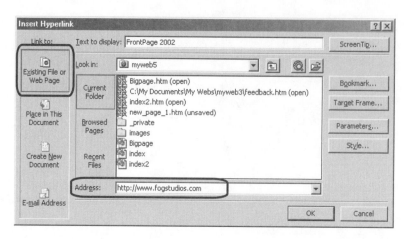

NOTE Other options available through the Insert Hyperlink dialog box are Bookmark, Target Frame (when you click a hyperlink on a page displayed in one frame on a Frames Page, the page the hyperlink points to usually opens another frame, designated the Target Frame), Parameters (access to additional hyperlink parameters), and Style (additional formatting options).

6. Click the **OK** button. You now return to Page view, where the link opens in blue.

TIP To remove a hyperlink, click the Page button on the Views bar, select the text or object with the hyperlink you want to remove, click Insert Hyperlink button on the Standard toolbar, and then click the Remove Link button.

Link to an E-mail Address

1. Open a page of your site in Page view.

2. Select the word or words you want to link from.

3. Click the **Insert Hyperlink** button 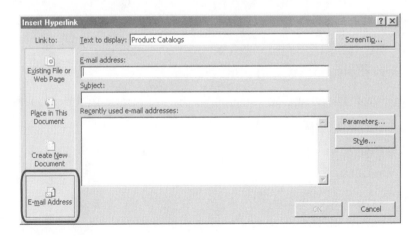 on the Standard toolbar. The Insert Hyperlink dialog box opens.

4. Click the **E-mail Address** button on the **Link To** bar. The words you entered as the link on your Web page appear in the **Text To Display** box.

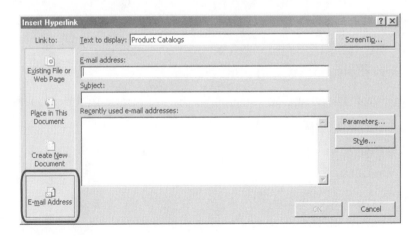

As you create more links of this type, they begin to appear in the Recently Used E-Mail Addresses box.

5. In the **Address** box, type the e-mail address you want to link to and the text you would like to automatically appear in the Subject line (optional).

6. Click the **OK** button to complete the link.

Internet Protocols and URLs

Communication on the Internet done by the Transmission Control Protocol/Internet Protocol (TCP/IP). The TCP determines how data files are split into packets for transmission through cyberspace, while the IP addresses make sure the packets are routed to the correct destination.

File Transfer Protocol (FTP) is the program that made the Internet accessible to everyone with a computer and modem.

When the web is in place, all its components are identified by their Uniform Resource Locator (URL). The entire address includes the Hypertext Transfer Protocol (HTTP), a colon, two forward slashes, and the site type (usually WWW). This is followed by the domain address (the site's name) followed by a period and the domain name (refers to the type of site). A sample URL for the HTTP server owned by the publisher of this book would be: http://www.sybex.com.

Previewing and Printing Web Pages

Printed pages are helpful when you are working in Preview view. Rather than toggling between a page in progress and a Browser Preview of that page, for example, you can print the Preview so that you have it in hard copy format. Printouts are also helpful when editing your pages. Before printing, you will want to preview the page to determine that there are no obvious errors.

Preview Web Pages

1. Choose **File** ➢ **Print Preview**. This opens a scaled-down image of the page you want to print and a series of buttons. The button choices are:

    ◇ **Print** button—Engages the printing process. The preview closes and the Print dialog box opens.

    ◇ **Next Page** button—Displays the next page in the sequence for multiple-page printing.

    ◇ **Previous Page** button—Takes you to the previous page in a sequence.

    ◇ **Two Page** button—Toggles between a single-page and a two-page spread in Preview mode.

    ◇ **Zoom In** button—Magnifies the preview image.

    ◇ **Zoom Out** button—Reduces the size of the characters to show more of the page preview.

❖ **Close** button—Shuts down the preview.

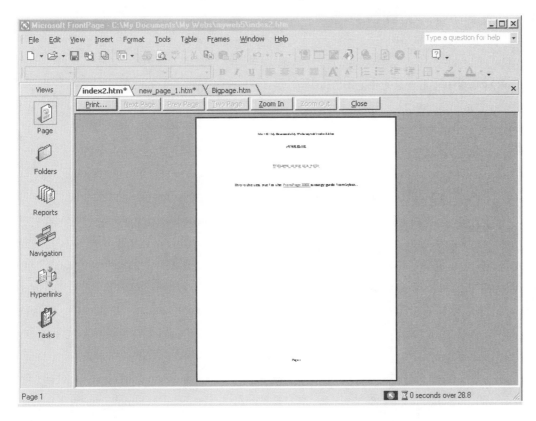

Print Web Pages

1. Choose **File** ➢ **Print**. The Print dialog box opens.

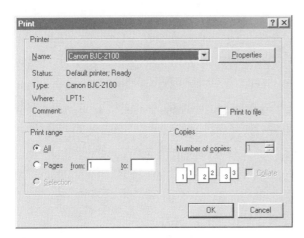

2. Select the print options you want.

3. Click the **OK** button.

Saving Web Pages

FrontPage simplifies the process of saving a web page in several different forms, all of which are accessible through the Save As dialog box.

Save a Web Page

1. Choose **File ➢ Save As**. The Save As dialog box opens.

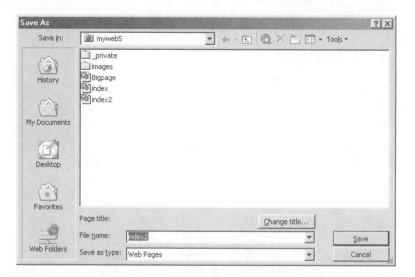

2. In the **File Name** box, enter the page name.

3. Click the **Look In** drop-down arrow ![arrow], and then select the folder location where you want to save the Web page.

4. Click the **Save As Type** drop-down arrow ![arrow] to display the following save options:

◇ **All Files** —use to save a complete web.

◇ **Web Pages**—save the selected file as a web page with a .htm extension.

◇ **FrontPage Template**—save the selected file as a template to be used for future FrontPage webs.

- ◊ **Active Server Pages**—save the selected file with a .asp extension.

- ◊ **Hypertext Template**—save the file as an HTML template.

- ◊ **Hypertext Style Sheet**—save the file as a cascading style sheet that can be used to apply themes to other pages.

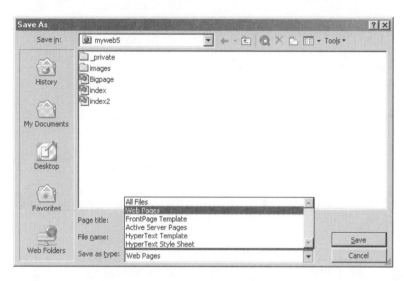

5. Select a format to save the Web site or page.

6. Click the **Save** button.

Importing Web Content

When you're working on a web, you might want to import a page file (or even an entire folder) that was created in another Microsoft program. Or you might want to download a site that you admire from the web so that you can analyze its structure closely before preparing your own.

Import Web Content

1. Click the **Folders** button on the Views bar.

2. Select the folder you want to import the file or folder to (if you're importing a picture, for example, target it to the Images folder).

3. Choose **File ➣ Import**. The Import dialog box opens.

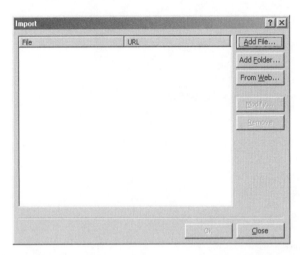

4. Click the **Add File** button. The Add File To Import List dialog box opens.

The Add Folder button functions exactly like the Add File button, except that you can then specify an entire folder of content to be imported to the web.

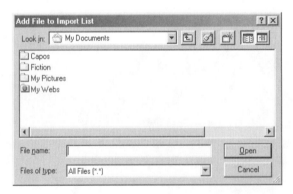

5. Click the **Look In** drop-down arrow ▼, and then select the location with file, Folder, or URL you want to import.

6. Double-click the file to add it to the Import dialog box.

7. When you have selected all the files that you want to import, click the **OK** button in the Import dialog box to complete the process.

Exporting Web Content

It is also possible to export one or more files from FrontPage to a location outside your web using the Export command or Copy and Paste commands. This process can be executed using the Folder List, Folders view, or Navigation view.

Export Content

1. Select the files or folders you want to copy.

2. Choose **File** ➢ **Export**. The Export Selected As dialog box opens.

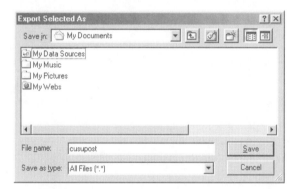

3. Click the **Save In** drop-down arrow [image], and then select the folder location where you want to export the Web content.

4. Click the **Save** button.

> **TIP** To export a file or folder under a new name, select the file or folder, then choose File ➢ Save, enter the new name and select a new location, and then click the Save button.

Export Content Using Copy and Paste

1. Select the files or folders you want to copy.

2. Click the **Copy** button 📋 on the Standard toolbar.

3. Display the location you want to move the content to.

4. Right-click the area where you want to place the content, and the click **Paste** on the shortcut menu. The source files or folders are copied into their new location.

3 Working with Web Page Text

Text and images are not only the meat and potatoes of web design; they are also the appetizer, vegetable, bread, butter, wine and dessert. The web is all about information. Although it can be presented in many multimedia forms including art, sound files, and movies, the basic building block of any Web site is the text. The object of web design is to create and manipulate alpha-numeric text and several types of graphics into a pleasing visual experience that communicates the presentation you intended. The best designs convey a sense of visual balance and coherency that only comes with practice and experience. But, it always helps to begin with a good set of tools. In this chapter, you will learn to enter and manipulate text as the foundation of your Web site.

Entering Text in a Page

There are two methods of entering text on a Web page: as part of a template or from scratch. When starting out, we strongly recommend that you work from a template. If you are working with templates, you can begin by editing the boilerplate text that opens as part of the template.

Click on the template text that you wish to replace and begin typing. The boilerplate text disappears and your text begins flowing into that section of the template. Be sure to constrain your text to the original area provided in the template and, if necessary, edit what you wish to say to make the copy fit within the allotted space.

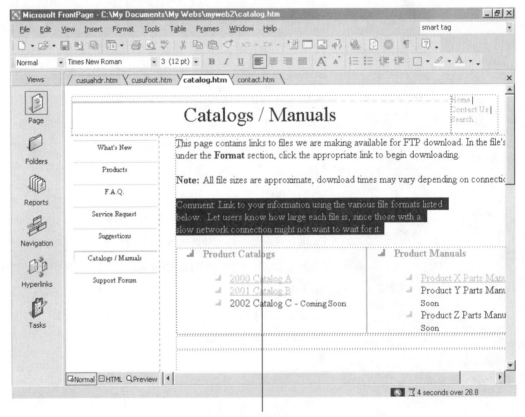

Boilerplate text in a template

| **TIP** | After you have highlighted the text you want replaced, it is not necessary to press the Delete key. You can begin typing and your new text automatically replaces the previous text. |

The other way to enter text is on a blank page. Create a new page, and start typing.

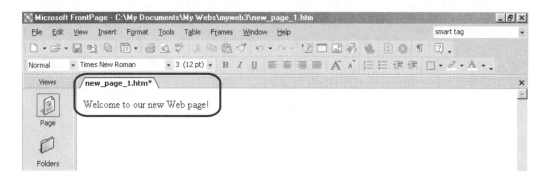

Selecting Text in a Page

Before you can edit or format text, you need to select, or highlight, the text you want to modify or change. Then you can delete, replace, move (cut), or copy text within one Web page or between Web pages.

Select Text

1. Select text using any of four methods.

- ◇ **Click-and-drag with the mouse**. Place your cursor at the beginning of the block of text you want to replace or move. Hold down the left mouse button and drag your cursor over the selected text until it is highlighted. Then release the mouse button.

- ◇ **Shift+Arrow keys**. Press the Shift key and continue to hold it while using the arrow keys to manipulate the text cursor until the selected portion is highlighted. The left and right arrow keys move the cursor one character at a time, while the up and down arrow keys move the cursor one line at a time.

- ◇ **Shift+Ctrl+Arrow keys**. Press Shift and Ctrl while using the arrow keys to highlight the selected text by moving the text cursor. The left and right arrows select text one word at a time; the up arrow highlights everything from the original position of the text cursor back to the beginning of the paragraph; and the down arrow selects all text from the original position of the text cursor to the end of the paragraph.

◇ **Shift+Ctrl+Home/End keys**. Press Shift and Ctrl and press Home to select everything from the original position of the text cursor back to the top of the page. Press Shift+Ctrl and End to highlight everything from the original position of the text cursor to the end of the page. Alternately, you can place the insertion point where you want to begin highlighting, then press and hold down the Shift key. Then click on the place where you want the highlighting to end, then release the Shift key.

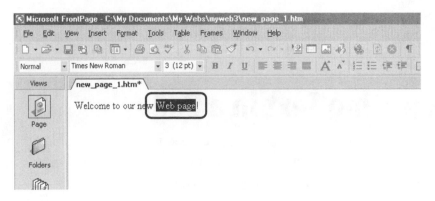

Moving and Copying Text

Drag-and-drop

A technique for moving or copying data short distances.

Text can be moved and copied in FrontPage just like in other word processing software. You can move or copy text within a Web page, between Web pages, or to another program. When you cut (for a move) or copy text or graphics, FrontPage places it on the Clipboard. To complete the copy or move, you paste the data stored on the Clipboard in another location. To copy or move text or graphics without using the Clipboard, you can use a technique called **drag-and-drop**. Drag-and-drop makes it easy to copy or move text or graphics short distances on your Web page.

Move or Copy Text

1. Select the text you want to move or copy.

2. To move the text from its current location, click the **Cut** button 🔏 on the Standard toolbar. The text is removed from its current location and placed on the Clipboard.

3. To copy the text to a new location, while leaving the original highlighted text in its current location, click the **Copy** button on the Standard toolbar. A copy of the text is placed on the Clipboard.

4. Click to position the insertion point where you wish either the cut or copied text to be inserted.

NOTE   You can cut or copy text between documents and even between FrontPage and other Microsoft programs. Switch between programs on the system taskbar at the bottom of the screen.

5. Click the **Paste** button on the Standard toolbar. The text is copied from the Clipboard to the new location, but also remains on the Clipboard for future placements.

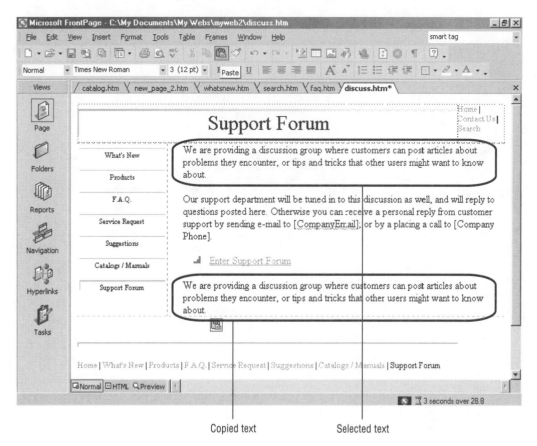

Copied text   Selected text

Smart tag

A button that helps you control the results of certain actions, such as copy and paste or automatic text correction.

6. After you paste an item, the **Paste Options** button appears next to the item on the Web page. You can click the Paste Options button to display a list of options on the shortcut menu. This button, known as a **smart tag**, allows you to immediately adjust how information is pasted or how automatic changes occur. Smart tags and their associated choices vary depending on the operation.

Move or Copy Text Using Drag-and-Drop

1. Select the text you want to move or copy.

2. To move the text from its current location, drag the selection to the new location, and then release the mouse button.

3. To copy the text to a new location, hold down the Ctrl key and drag the selection to the new location, and then release the mouse button.

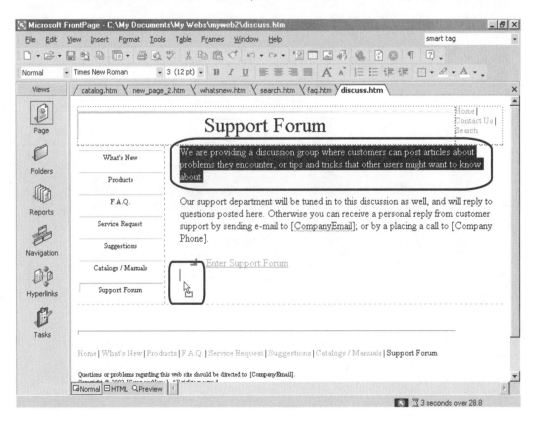

Working with the Office Clipboard

If you are going to do repeated cut, copy and paste operations, it is a good idea to first open the Office Clipboard. With Office XP, you can use the **Office Clipboard** to store multiple pieces of information from several different sources in one storage area that is shared by all Office programs. When you copy multiple items or choose the Office Clipboard command on the Edit menu, the Clipboard task pane opens, showing the items within it. You can paste these pieces of information into any Office program, either individually or all at once.

Office Clipboard

A temporary area that holds up to 24 pieces of copied information and is available from within any Office program.

Move or Copy Text Using the Clipboard

1. Choose **Edit ➤ Office Clipboard**. The Clipboard task pane opens.

2. Perform cut, copy and paste operations in accordance with the steps of the previous section. You can place up to 24 items on the Clipboard.

3. To copy items from the Clipboard into the document, click to position the insertion point, and then click the text on the Clipboard. The Clipboard item is inserted into the document.

> **TIP**   You can paste items from the Clipboard one at a time, or paste all of the contents by clicking Paste All at the top of the Clipboard.

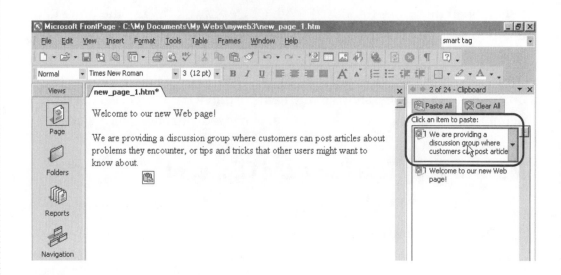

> **NOTE**   To delete items in the Clipboard, click the drop-down arrow next to the item you want to delete, and then click Delete.

Creating Bulleted and Numbered Lists

The best way to draw attention to a list is to format the items with bullets or numbers. For different emphasis, you can change any bullet or number style to one of the predefined formats. You can also customize the list style or insert a picture as a bullet. If you move, insert, or delete items in a numbered list, FrontPage sequentially renumbers the list for you. The capability to generate bulleted and numbered lists is essential to the creation of most webs. Both types of these lists are generated in Page view.

Create Bulleted and Numbered Lists

1. Click the **Page** button on the Views bar.

2. Choose **Format** ➢ **Bullets and Numbering**. The Bullets and Numbering dialog box opens. If you are using a Theme, the Plain Bullets tab is
unavailable. **Picture Bullets** is the default setting and the dialog box
will use the design of those specified by the Theme.

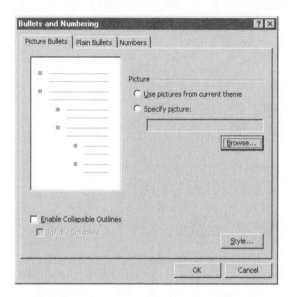

3. To switch to other types of bulleted lists, click the **Plain Bullets** tab
and click on one of four templates to select it.

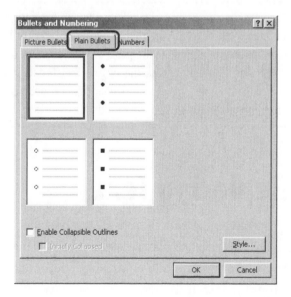

4. To switch to numbered lists, click the **Numbers** tab and click on one of six templates to select it.

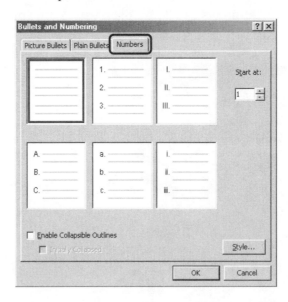

5. After you have made your selection, click the **OK** button to insert the first bullet onto your page. Type the first entry and then press the Enter key.

Every time you press the Enter key, a new bullet will appear. To end a list, press Enter twice.

NOTE If you're feeling ambitious, you can create your own bullet, using any graphics program. When you've produced your custom bullet, save it, preferably in either GIF (.gif) or JPEG (.jpg) format. In FrontPage, place the insertion point at the place where you want to start the list. Choose Format ➢ Bullets And Numbering, click the Picture Bullets tab, click the Specify Picture option button, click the Browse button to locate your creation, double-click a picture, and then click the OK button. You can proceed as you would with any other bullet style.

Finding and Replacing Text

Suppose that you discover you have misspelled or want to change a word throughout an entire Web page. You do not need to read through the document to find every instance of the word and manually change it. The Find and Replace commands can do that for you. If the word you want to change extends across fifty pages, you can still make the change without having to edit fifty individual pages. FrontPage can find every instance for you, and walk you through the Web site from page to page until all the corrections have been made.

Find and Replace Text on a Web Page

1. Choose **Edit** ➢ **Find**. The Find and Replace dialog box opens.

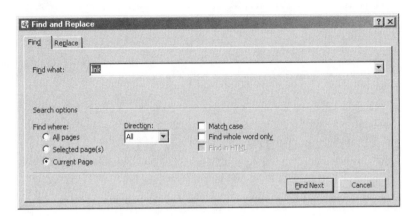

2. In the **Find What** box, enter the text for which you are searching, and then click the **Replace** tab.

3. In the **Replace** box, enter the replacement text.

4. Define the parameters of your search (All Pages, Selected Pages, Current Page, Match Case, Find Whole Word Only, etc.), and then select one of the following buttons:

- ❖ **Replace All** button. Replaces all instances of the text.

- ❖ **Replace** button. Replaces the selected instance of the text.

- ❖ **Find Next** button. Locates the next instance of the text.

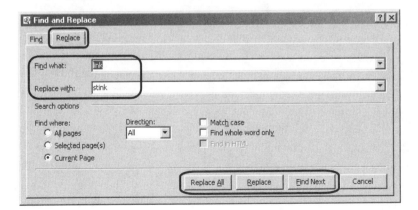

4. When you're done, click the **Cancel** button to close the Find and Replace dialog box.

> **NOTE**   You can also choose certain filters to help your search once you have opened the Find And Replace dialog box. Either select or deselect certain check boxes, such as the Match Case or Find Whole Word Only check boxes. You locate text on a case-sensitive basis via the Match Case check box. A match will be found only if the same letters are upper- and lower-case

Find and Replace Text on a Web Site

1. Click the **Folders** button on the Views bar.

2. Choose **Edit ➢ Find**. The Find and Replace dialog box opens.

3. In the **Find What** box, enter the text for which you are searching, and then click the **Replace** tab.

4. In the **Replace** box, enter the replacement text.

5. Click the **Selected Pages** option button, and then click the **Find In Web** button. The list of pages containing the selected word(s) opens.

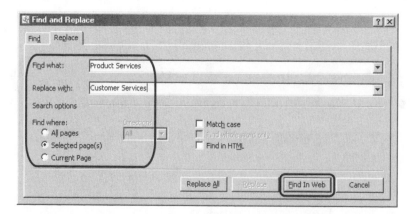

6. While holding down the Ctrl key, click the specific pages you want searched. Otherwise, the program will search all pages.

7. When FrontPage lists the pages in which the text you're seeking was found (step four), you can open any of these pages in Page view by double-clicking the page from the list. The first instance of the text you're looking for is highlighted. This text can be replaced via the **Replace** command.

8. When you're finished, you are prompted to close the current document before moving on to the next. If changes were made, your page will be automatically saved.

Formatting Text

You'll often want to format, or change the style of text to add emphasis to part of a Web page. **Boldface**, *italics*, <u>underlines</u>, and other text effects are toggle switches, which means you simply click to turn them on and off. For special emphasis, you can apply multiple formats, such as bold and italics. You can also change the font typeface and size. Using one font typeface for headings and another for main text adds a professional look to your Web page.

Format Text Quickly

1. In the Page view, select the text you want to format.

2. Click a formatting button (such as Bold, Italic, or Underline) on the Formatting toolbar to apply the attribute that you want the selected text. You can continue apply attributes as long as you select the text.

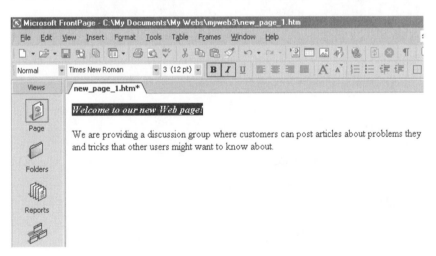

Change the Font or Size of Text Quickly

1. In Page view, select the text you want to format.

2. Click the **Font** drop-down arrow ▼ or the **Font Size** drop-down arrow ▼ on the Formatting toolbar, and then click a font typeface or point size.

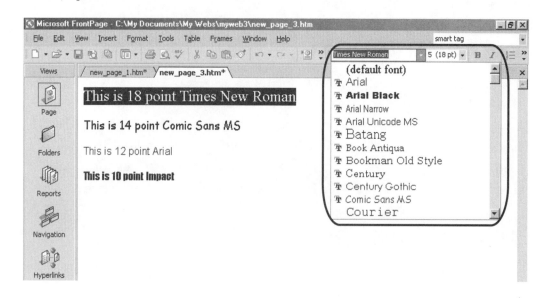

Format Text Using the Font Dialog Box

1. In Page view, select the text you want to format.

2. Choose **Format** ➢ **Font**. The Font dialog box opens.

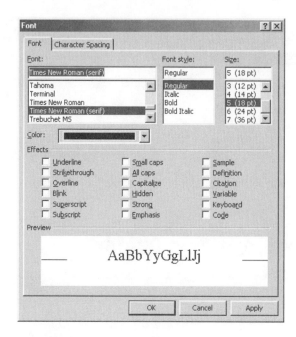

3. Click the **Font** tab, if necessary.

4. Select the formatting options you want.

- ◇ In the **Font** box, select a font.

- ◇ In the **Font Style** box, select a font style.

- ◇ In the **Size** text box, select a font size.

- ◇ On the **Color** drop-down list, select a font color.

- ◇ Under **Effects**, select the effect of your choice, if any.

5. Click the **OK** button.

Setting Text Alignment and Spacing

Text alignments vary the look of a Web page and help lead the user through the text. You can align text along the left or right margin, in the center, or equally across the page. You can quickly change text alignment using alignment buttons on the Formatting toolbar. Line spacing is another way to vary the look of a Web page. The lines in a Web page are single-spaced by default, but you can easily change line spacing to double or 1.5 lines to allow extra space between every line. Sometimes, you'll want to add space above and below certain paragraphs, such as for headlines or indented quotations to help set off the text.

Change Text Alignment

1. In Page view, select the text you want to align.

2. Click an alignment button on the Formatting toolbar to apply the attribute that you want the selected text.

- ◇ **Align Left** button ≣. Aligns text along the left margin. The text is uneven along the right margin.

- ◇ **Center** button ≣. Aligns text in the middle of the page.

- ◇ **Align Right** button ≣. Aligns text along the right margin. The text is uneven along the left margin.

- ◇ **Justify** button ≣. Aligns text evenly between the two margins.

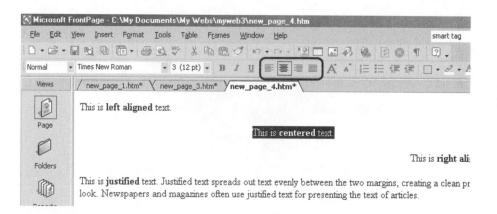

Change Line Spacing

1. In Page view, select the paragraph you want to change.

2. Choose **Format** ➢ **Paragraph**. The Paragraph dialog box opens.

3. Click the **Line Spacing** drop-down arrow ▾, and then click the spacing you want.

4. In the **Before** box, type the space you want to add above each selected paragraph (in points).

5. In the **After** box, type the space you want to add below each selected paragraph (in points).

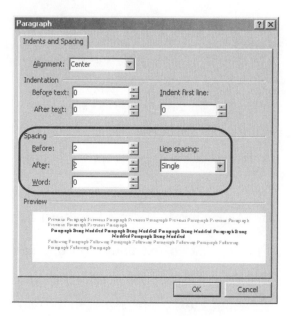

6. Click the **OK** button.

Change Paragraph Indents

1. In Page view, select the paragraph you want to change.

2. Choose **Format** ➤ **Paragraph**. The Paragraph dialog box opens.

3. In the **Before Text** box, type the space you want before the selected paragraph (in points).

4. In the **After Text** box, type the space you want after the selected paragraph (in points).

5. In the **Indent First Line** box, type the space you want before the first line of the selected paragraph (in points).

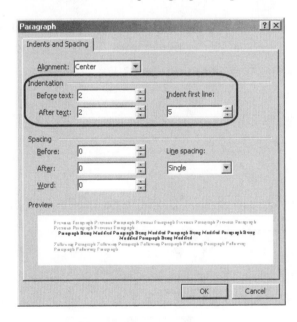

6. Click the **OK** button.

Style

A collection of formatting characteristics identified by a single name.

Built-In Style

The formatting attributes available to you by default in the FrontPage Style list.

User-Defined Style

A style that is at least partially designed by a user.

Cascading Style Sheet (CSS)

A document you use to maintain a consistent style throughout multiple Web pages and that gives you greater control over how your web is displayed in different browsers.

Embedded CSS

When you create a new page, or modify the existing style of a page, FrontPage automatically creates an embedded CSS that contains all the code stored between the page's HTML tags.

External CSS

Style sheets that can be linked to several Web pages so that you can apply a single style consistently throughout an entire web. If you make an alteration in your style, it only needs to be changed in the External CSS and the whole site automatically is updated. Most External CSS carry .css file extensions.

Inline CSS

User-defined styles that are applied to a single-page element. This is the rarest type of CSS.

Creating Headings and Subheadings

The question of headings and subheadings are all issues of **Style**. Style elements can be applied to a variety of page components in FrontPage, including text, graphics, and tables. It also offers you **Built-In Style**, or allows you to generate your own **User-Defined Style**, complete with the formatting attributes of **Cascading Style Sheets**.

Cascading Style Sheets are becoming the predominant method of formatting a Web site. A CSS contains style definitions, called Selectors, which are the HTML components linked to a specialized list of style properties and values. A selector is followed by those properties and values. For example, H1 {font-size: x-large; color: green}, H2 {font-size: large; color: blue). H1 and H2 are selectors that modify the formatting properties of standard HTML tags.

There are three types of Cascading Style Sheets in FrontPage: **embedded**, **external**, and the rarely-used **inline**. Both built-in and user-defined styles from the same style list are used when you're editing a page.

Apply a Style to Text

1. In Page view, select the text you want to change into a heading or subheading.

2. Click the **Style** drop-down arrow ▾ on the Formatting toolbar.

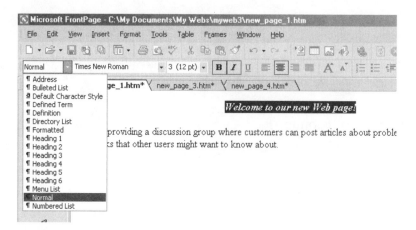

3. Click a style (such as Heading 1, Heading 2, etc.) from the drop-down list.

Create a Style to Text

1. Click the **Page** button on the Views bar.

2. Choose **Format** ➢ **Style**. The Style dialog box opens.

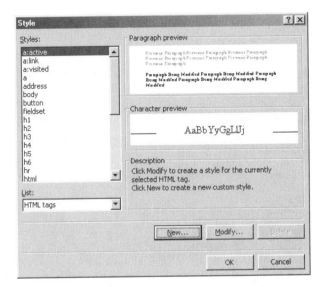

3. Click the **New** button. The New Style dialog box opens.

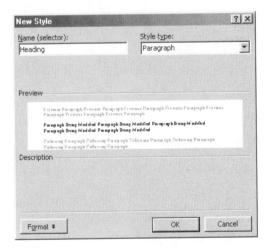

4. Click the **New** button. The New Style dialog box opens.

5. In the **Name (Selector)** box, type a name for the style.

6. Click the **Style Type** drop-down arrow 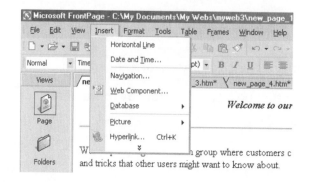, and then click **Paragraph** to include the selected text's line spacing and margins in the style, or click **Character** to include only formatting, such as font, size, and bold, in the style.

7. Click the **Format** button, and then click a formatting command to include additional formatting to the style.

8. Click the **OK** button, and then click the **OK** button again.

> **TIP** To modify a style, choose Format ➤ Style, select the style you want to change, click the Modify button, make changes to the style, click the OK button, and then click the OK button again.

Adding Horizontal Lines

Horizontal lines have a variety of uses in the construction of a web. Whether they're used to separate sections of a page or to underline an important piece of text, you have several decisions to make. Lines have a variety of properties that you can modify, including width, height, alignment, and color. If a theme has already been applied to the page, the line is changed by the theme's properties.

Add a Horizontal Line

1. In Page view, move the insertion point to the location where you want the horizontal line inserted.

2. Choose **Insert** ➤ **Horizontal Line**. The line is inserted into the document.

Modify a Horizontal Line

1. Open the Web page with the horizontal line you want to change.

2. Double-click the horizontal line you want to modify. The Horizontal Line Properties dialog box opens.

3. Select the formatting options you want.

◇ **Width**—Width of the line. Specified in pixels or as a percentage of the window width.

◇ **Height**—Height of the line in pixels.

◇ **Alignment**—Alignment of the line on the page.

◇ **Color**—Color of the line, unless you want it shaded. If you select a color, shading is no longer an option.

◇ **Solid Line**—Check this box and the line opens solid. Don't check it and the line opens shaded.

4. Click the **OK** button.

TIP   If a theme has been applied to a page, you can only change the line's alignment.

Checking Spelling

Using FrontPage, you can correct spelling errors on a Web site immediately, or create a task for each page with an error and correct them later. Begin by opening the page whose spelling you want to examine. If you commonly use words unique to a hobby or profession that would not appear in a normal dictionary, or are unlikely to be part of the common vernacular, consider adding them to your dictionary so that they will not repeatedly be called into question during spell checks.

> **TIP** To check your spelling as you type, choose Tools ➤ Page Options, click the General tab, click the Check Spelling As You Type check box to select it. Words the online dictionary doesn't recognize are underlined with a wavy line. Right-click the word that is underlined to open the shortcut menu. When FrontPage learns the spellings of words you use regularly, it even automatically corrects some errors as you type.

Check Spelling in a Web Page

1. Click the **Page** button on the Views bar.

2. Place the insertion point at the place in the document where you want to begin the check for spelling mistakes.

3. Choose **Tools** ➤ **Spelling**. The program begins scanning the document for words that aren't in its dictionary. When it locates a word, it will offer suggested alternative spellings, or you can choose to ignore the selection. The Spelling dialog box opens.

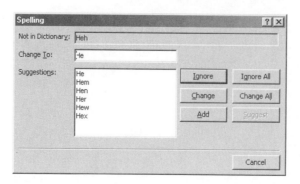

4. To replace the misspelled word with a word from the Suggestions list, click the suggested word, and then click the **Change** button. Click the **Change All** button to correct all instances of the word.

5. To correct the word yourself, type the correct word in the **Change To** box, and then click the **Change** button. Click the **Change All** button to correct all instances of this word.

6. If the unrecognized word is correctly spelled but the program doesn't know it (as with a name, for example), click the **Ignore** button to ignore this instance of the word, or click the **Ignore All** button to ignore all instances of this word.

7. Click the **Add** button to add this word to your custom dictionary.

8. When the spell checker reaches the end of the document, if it hasn't searched the beginning, a prompt will ask if you want it to resume the search at the start of the document.

Spell Checking in a Web Site

1. Click the **Folders** button on the Views bar.

2. Select the pages in the Web site you want to check. Click the first page to check, and then press and hold down the Ctrl key while clicking the other pages you want examined for spelling.

3. Choose **Tools ➢ Spelling**. The Spelling dialog box opens.

4. To check spelling in all of the pages in the current Web site, click the **Entire Web** option button in the Spelling dialog box.

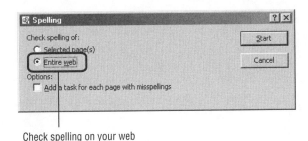

Check spelling on your web

5. To check spelling in pages you have selected, click the **Selected Page(s)** option button in the Spelling dialog box.

> **NOTE** If you want FrontPage to add a task for each page with misspelled words, click the Add a Task for Each Page with Misspellings check box to select it in the Spelling dialog box. By assigning spelling corrections to Tasks, you can come back and correct them at your convenience.

6. Click the **Start** button. The Spelling dialog box lists the pages with misspelled words.

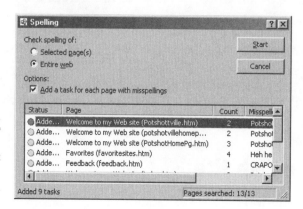

7. Double-click the first misspelled word in the list. If a misspelled word needs to be corrected, the Spelling dialog box opens. Otherwise, the Continue With The Next Page? dialog box opens.

8. To correct a misspelled word, use the buttons in the Spelling dialog to change or ignore the misspelled word. To continue spell checking the next page, click the **Next Page** button.

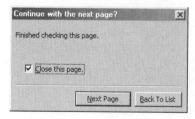

9. If you want to stop the spell check or it is done checking all the pages, click the **Back To List** button.

10. Click the **Cancel** button to close the Spelling dialog box.

Finding the Right Words

Repeating the same word in a Web page can reduce a message's effectiveness. Instead, replace some words with synonyms, words with similar meanings, or find antonyms, words with opposite meanings. If you need help finding exactly the right word, you can use the Thesaurus.

Use the Thesaurus

1. In Page view, select the word you want to look up.

2. Choose **Tools** ➤ **Thesaurus**. The Thesaurus dialog box opens.

3. Click a word to display its synonyms and antonyms.

4. Click the word you want to use.

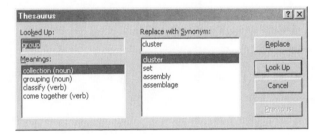

5. Click the **Replace** button.

6. Click **Cancel** to close the dialog box.

Applying XML Formatting

XML, or Extensible Markup Language, is an alternative to HTML. This format is ideal for producing extensive, highly-structured data from an application in a consistent manner. The difference between XML and HTML is subtle but profound: XML describes a web document's content, while HTML tags describe how the document looks. HTML tags assign certain characteristics to the text they surround. XML is ideal for data-intensive web environments and, unlike HTML, supports customized tags for specific data. XML tags, however, employ a much tighter rule system with regard to XML syntax. So much as a single missing tag or mis-formatted attributes makes the entire document unreadable.

Apply XML Formatting

1. In the Page view, click the **HTML** tab at the bottom of the window.

2. In the HTML pane, right-click anywhere on the page, and then click **Apply XML Formatting Rules**. FrontPage scans the XML code for missing or incomplete tags.

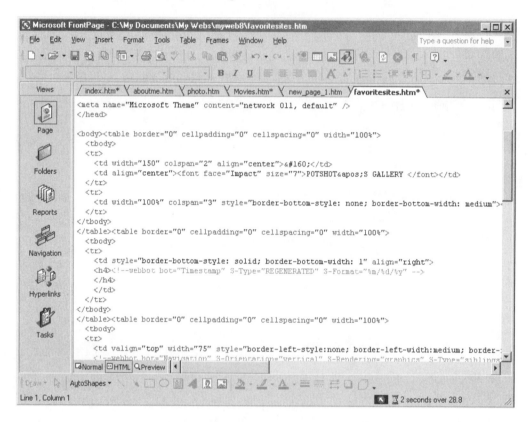

Inserting WordArt Text

WordArt

Text objects that you create with pre-defined effects.

To add life to your document, you can add a **WordArt** object to your document. WordArt is a feature that allows you to add visual enhancements to your text that go beyond changing a font or font size. You can select a WordArt style that stretches your text horizontally, vertically, or diagonally. You can also change the character spacing and reshape the text. WordArt is an object that you can move, resize, or even rotate. Text in WordArt does not wrap or need margin settings, because the text is an object.

Insert WordArt Text

1. Click the **Insert WordArt** button 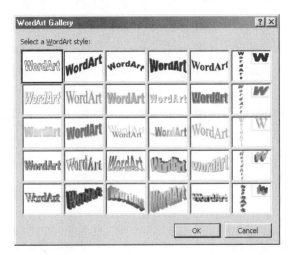 on the Drawing toolbar. The WordArt Gallery dialog box opens.

2. Click the **WordArt** effect you want, and then click the **OK** button. The Edit WordArt Text dialog box opens.

3. In the **Text** box, type the text you want.

4. Select the formatting options you want to apply to the text.

   ◆ To change the font type, click the **Font** drop-down arrow, and then select a font.

   ◆ To change the font size, click the **Size** drop-down arrow, and then select a size.

   ◆ To make text bold, click the **Bold** button **B**.

   ◆ To make text italic, click the **Italic** button *I*.

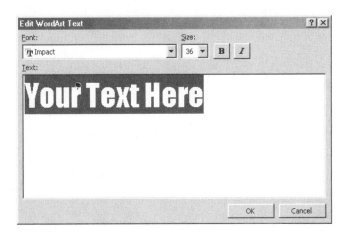

5. Click the **OK** button to close the Edit WordArt Text dialog box.

Inserting Text with Handwriting

When you first install an Office XP program, the Office Language toolbar appears at the top of the screen. The Office Language toolbar allows you to dictate text or insert handwritten text into a Web page. You can use your mouse or stylus to write (using cursive style, printing, or a hybrid of both) and insert the handwritten text into a Web page. Although you can use the mouse, for best results, you should use a handwriting input device. The program recognizes the handwriting when there is enough text for it to do so, when you reach the end of the line, or if you pause for about two seconds.

> **NOTE** To minimize the toolbar, click the minus sign at the right end of the toolbar. The Language toolbar will dock in the System taskbar at the bottom right of the screen. If you are using English as the default language, the toolbar will be denoted by the letters EN (other languages have appropriate abbreviations as well). To restore the toolbar to the top of the screen, click the icon, and then click Show The Language Bar from the shortcut menu.

Insert Hand Written Text on a Writing Pad

1. Place the insertion point in the exact position on your Web page where you want to transmit the handwriting.

2. If the Language toolbar is not available on the screen, right-click the **EN** button on the right side of the taskbar near the clock, and then click **Show The Language Bar**. The Language toolbar opens.

3. Click the **Handwriting** button on the Language toolbar, and then click **Writing Pad**. The Writing Pad dialog box opens.

To increase or decrease the size of the Writing Pad dialog box, move the pointer to one of the dialog box's outside edges until a diagonal, double-sided arrow appears, then drag the corner until the box is the size you want.

4. Move the insertion point into the Writing Pad dialog box. When the cursor changes into a pen, you've entered a writing area.

To enter handwriting in the program immediately without waiting for a recognition delay, click the Recognize Now button on the Writing Pad dialog box.

5. To actually write, use a handwriting input device (such as a drawing tablet), or move your mouse on your mouse pad to form words. The Writing Pad can be used as a guide. Write on the line, as you would use the lines on notebook paper. Your handwriting will be entered at the insertion point in the program.

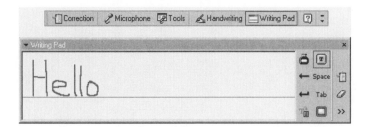

Instead of using the Writing Pad, you can also write directly on the page using the Write Anywhere command. To write directly on the page, click Handwriting on the Language toolbar, and then click Write Anywhere. The Write Anywhere toolbar opens. Move the mouse over a blank area of your Web page, and then write your text. The handwritten words are converted to text on your screen.

6. To close the handwriting box, click the **Close** button ☒ on the Writing Pad.

NOTE   Automatic recognition can be toggled on or off. You can also change the rate at which hand-writing is recognized, or the pen color and width. Click the Options button in the upper-left corner of the Writing Pad dialog box or the Write Anywhere toolbar, and then click Options to access these settings.

---

4 Working with Web Page Graphics

Now that you've explored the world of text, it is time for you to turn your attention to the other part of web content—graphics! In this chapter you will learn how to insert new graphics on pages. You will also learn to crop, resize, animate and copy graphics, and even how to add special effects so that your web has a look that really sizzles. By the end of this chapter you will even know how to add hyperlinks to graphics, and work with hotspots, which are invisible areas on a graphic, text block, or other web area to which a hyperlink has been assigned.

Understanding Graphics

Graphics can be used to provide visual interest, supplemental information, or even to support a theme. Whether it's the company logo on a business site or a special photo on your personal site, graphics brighten up a web. Graphics can be used in a variety of ways in FrontPage. For example, you can use a graphic element as a background. There are company logos for business sites, banner graphics, special bullets, link bars with navigation buttons, and so forth.

The most common formats for graphics are GIF (up to 256 colors) and JPEG (more than 256 colors). Both formats have specific strengths and weaknesses. With GIF format graphics, for example, you can designate one of your 256 or fewer colors as transparent, while JPEG is better suited to pictures containing thousands, or even millions of colors. You can also determine the level of file compression by resetting the graphic quality. The lower you set the quality, the higher the file compression and the smaller the file size.

There are several other graphic formats, including:

◆ BMP (Bitmap Format, the native Microsoft Windows format supports graphics up to 24-bits)

◆ TIFF (Tagged Image File Format, a high-resolution, tag-based file format)

◆ TGA (Truevision Targa Graphics Adaptor, which supports 1- to 32-bit graphics and boasts several professional-level features)

◆ RAS (Raster format, lightly compressed, it supports graphics up to 36-bit)

◆ EPS (Encapsulated PostScript file format, it enables PostScript graphics files to be integrated into other documents)

◆ PNG (Portable Network Graphics, a GIF alternative that supports transparency for multiple colors)

◆ WMF (Microsoft Windows Metafile, which supports bitmapped vector and EPS data).

When you save a graphic in a file format other than GIF or JPEG, FrontPage converts the file to GIF format if it has 8 bits of color or less, or to JPEG if it has more than 8 bits of color. At the more ambitious end of this graphic spectrum, you encounter animated GIF files and even videos. An animated GIF is a sequential display of GIF graphics.

Inserting Graphics

FrontPage makes it possible for you to insert graphics, pictures, scanned photographs, or artwork you scanned or created in a drawing program. All scanned graphics and photographs are bitmaps. Bitmap pictures are often saved with a .bmp, .png, .jpg, or .gif extension. You can also insert clip art from the Microsoft Clip Organizer that comes with all Office XP programs. For example, you can insert clip art graphics of scenic backgrounds, maps, buildings, or people. To insert a graphic, you use the Picture submenu on the Insert menu to specify the source—from a file, scanner or camera, or clip art gallery.

Insert Graphics from a File

1. In Page view, position the insertion point where you want to insert a graphic.

2. Choose **Insert** ➢ **Picture** ➢ **From File**. The Picture dialog box opens.

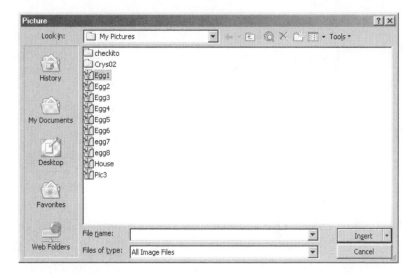

> **TIP** To preview pictures in the Picture dialog box, click the Views button drop-down arrow, and then click Preview.

3. Click the **Look In** drop-down arrow, and then select the folder location of the file you want to insert.

4. Click the file you want to insert, and then click the **Insert** button.

When you save the page, FrontPage prompts you to save the graphic to your Web site. Click the Yes button and the graphic will be placed in your Images folder. Graphics comprising 256 distinct colors or less are converted to GIF format. All other graphics are converted to JPEG format.

Insert Graphics from the Web

1. In Page view, position the insertion point where you want to insert a graphic.

2. Choose **Insert** ➢ **Picture** ➢ **From File**. The Picture dialog box opens.

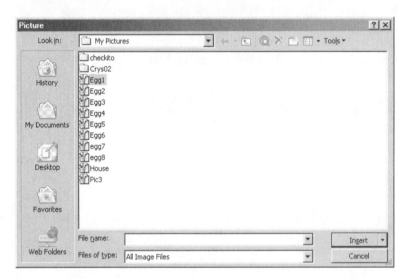

3. Click the **Search The Web** button . You will be transported, by default, to your Web browser, from which you may either conduct a search or simply enter the URL of the site containing the graphic you want to use.

When you copy material from the Web, you need to get permission from the owner to use it. In many cases, the Web site provides conditions of use.

4. Search the Web as you normally would using your browser.

5. When you locate the graphic you want to use, right-click the graphic, and then click **Copy**.

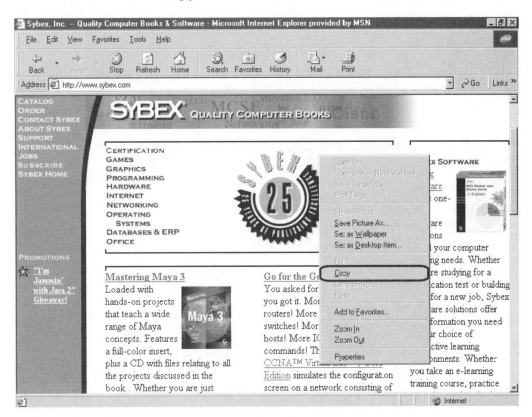

TIP If you are using Netscape Navigator 4.x or later, right-click the graphic, click Copy Graphic Location on the shortcut menu, then switch back to FrontPage, and paste over the text in the URL box.

6. Close your browser and switch back to FrontPage.

7. In Page view, right-click the location where you want to place the graphic, and then click **Paste** from the shortcut menu to add the graphic to your page. This inserts a reference on your page to the graphic on the Web site.

Insert Graphics from Clip Art

It is also possible to add **clip art** to your webs by way of FrontPage's Clip Organizer. Using the Clip Organizer you can preview art, graphics, and even videos before selecting the appropriate item to spice up your Web page.

Clip art
Pre-drawn art that can be taken from a commercial source and inserted into your web.

1. In Page view, position the insertion point at the location where you want the graphic inserted.

2. Choose **Insert ➢ Picture ➢ Clip Art**. The Insert Clip Art task pane opens.

When you first open the Insert Clip Art task pane, the Add Clips to Organizer dialog box also opens. Organizing your clip art, sound and movie clips will save you time if you are going to be doing considerable Web work with them, but you can perform the operation now or later at your discretion.

3. In the **Search text** box, type a word or phrase that describes the clip you want, and click the **Search** button.

4. In the **Results** list, click the clip you want to insert in your web.

5. Click the **Close** button ☒ in the Insert Clip Art task pane.

Insert Graphics from a Scanner or Camera

1. In Page view, position the insertion point where you want to insert the graphic.

2. Choose **Insert ➣ Picture ➣ From Scanner Or Camera**. The Insert Picture from Scanner or Camera dialog box opens.

> **NOTE** Check the instructions that come with your digital camera or scanner to make sure it is set up correctly and is compatible with FrontPage.

3. Click the **Device** drop-down arrow ▾, and then select the actual device you will be using to add a graphic.

> **NOTE** Only devices that have been previously installed on your system will appear in the listing of cameras and scanners.

4. Depending on the type of device, you might have to set the resolution level (either **Web Quality** or **Print Quality**) in this dialog box.

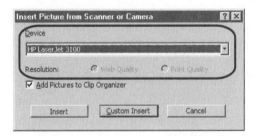

5. If you want to make the graphic easily accessible for future use, click the **Add Pictures To Clip Organizer** check box to select it.

6. Click the **Insert** button or the **Custom Insert** button, depending on your device and FrontPage will synchronize with and initialize the device.

7. Follow the directions provided for your specific device to complete the insertion.

Cropping and Resizing Graphics

Cropping
The process of framing a portion of a photo and eliminating any unnecessary visual elements.

Cropping and resizing of graphics can be accomplished in FrontPage. If, for example, you have a photo of someone, but much of the picture is blurry, except for the subject's head, you can crop out everything except the non-blurry part and produce a fine head shot. It's possible to resize graphics, using both numerical and graphic-direct techniques.

> **NOTE**   If the Pictures Toolbar doesn't open when you select a graphic, choose View ➤ Toolbars ➤ Pictures.

Crop a Graphic

1. In Page view, select the graphic you want to crop. Resize handles appear on the graphic and the Picture toolbar opens.

2. Click the **Crop** button ⌗ on the Pictures toolbar. A cropping box appears inside the graphic.

3. Drag a resize handle on the cropping box to include the part of the graphic that you want to keep.

Cropping box

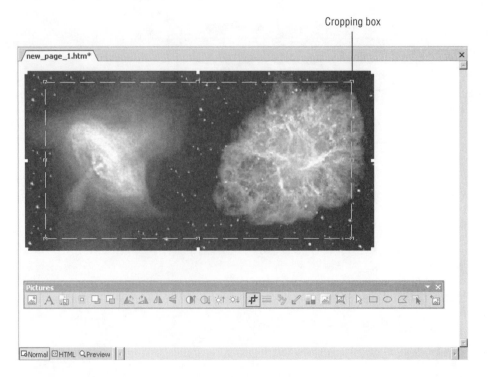

4. Click the **Crop** button 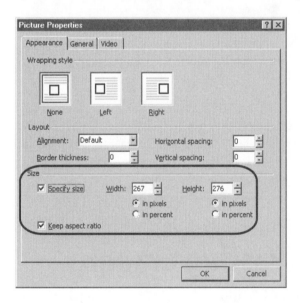 on the Pictures toolbar again to eliminate the area outside of the cropping box.

Resize Graphics Numerically

1. In Page view, right-click the graphic, and then click **Picture Properties** on the shortcut menu. The Picture Properties dialog box opens.

2. Click the **Appearance** tab.

3. Click the **Specify Size** check box to select it.

4. If you want to preserve the height-to-width proportions of the picture, click the **Keep Aspect Ratio** check box to select it. The aspect ratio refers to the proportions of a graphic. If you select this option, you only need to change the width or height, not both.

5. Decide whether you want to change the size in pixels or in percentage, and then enter values in the **Width** and **Height** boxes.

6. Click the **OK** button. The graphic is resized according to your specifications.

Resize Graphics Directly

1. In Page view, select the graphic you want to crop. Resize handles appear on the graphic and the Picture toolbar opens.

2. Drag a resize handle (small squares) to the size you want. To resize a graphic while preserving its proportions (that is, its aspect ration), drag a handle located in the graphic's corners diagonally.

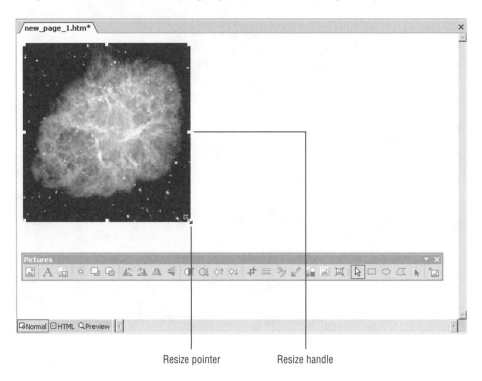

Resize pointer   Resize handle

> **TIP** To resize a thumbnail graphic that is part of a photo gallery, go to Page view. Choose Insert ➤ Web Component. In the Insert Web Component dialog box, double-click Photo Gallery, and then click the thumbnail you want to resize. Under Thumbnail Size, designate the new height and width in terms of pixels.

Copying and Pasting Graphics

Copying and pasting objects is another integral part of web design. You copy and paste graphics in the same way in which you copy and paste text.

Copy and Paste a Graphic

1. Select the AutoShape, WordArt, Clip Art or Picture you want to copy.

2. Click the **Copy** button on the Standard toolbar. The graphic remains in its original position and a copy is put on the Clipboard.

NOTE To move a graphic, use the Cut button on the Standard toolbar. When you use the Cut command, the graphic is removed from its current position and put on the Clipboard.

3. In FrontPage, in the Normal pane, click the position where you want the item to appear.

4. Click the **Paste** button on the Standard toolbar. The graphic is inserted in the new location.

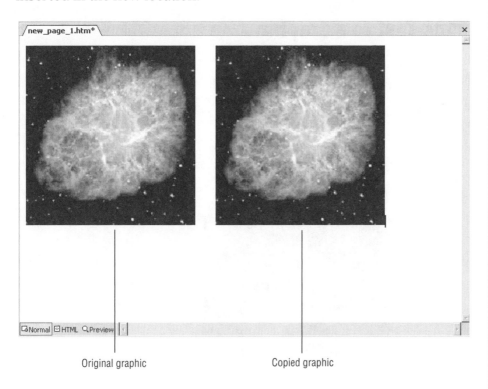

Original graphic　　　　　　　Copied graphic

NOTE The available options depend on the type of content you are pasting, the program you are pasting from, and the format of the text in the area where you are pasting.

Applying Special Effects to Graphics

You can apply what are designated as special effects to a graphic element. Text can be added; brightness and contrast can be adjusted, grayscale and wash out effects can be employed, and borders can surround the item and even produce a raised, 3-D effect. You can choose one color in a graphic to become transparent, as well as rotate and flip graphic elements clockwise or counter-clockwise. You can, in short, add a variety of effects to graphics.

NOTE   If the Pictures Toolbar doesn't open when you select a graphic, choose View ➢ Toolbars ➢ Pictures.

TIP   If you make several changes to a graphic that you don't want to keep, you can click the Restore button on the Pictures toolbar to return the graphic back to it's original state.

Add Text to a Graphic

1. In Page view, select the graphic in which you want to add text. Resize handles appear on the graphic and the Picture toolbar opens.

2. Click the **Text** button A on the Pictures toolbar. A text box opens on the graphic.

3. Enter your text in the box that is displayed on the graphic.

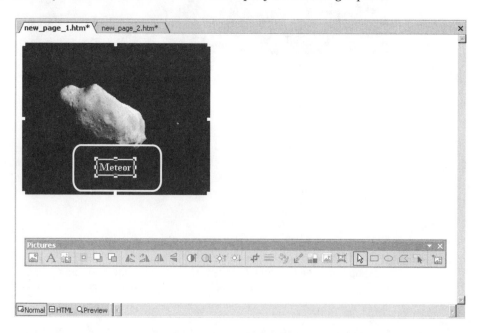

4. Choose **Format** ➢ **Font**. The Font dialog box opens, allowing you to select the formatting options you want to use.

5. To resize the text box, select the text box, and then drag one of the resize handles. You have accessed a resize handle when your cursor becomes a double-pointed arrow.

6. To move the text box, select the text box, and then drag the text box.

Adjust Graphic Contrast and Brightness

You can also increase or decrease the brightness of a graphic, as well as the color contrast.

1. In Page view, select the graphic you want to adjust. Resize handles appear on the graphic and the Picture toolbar opens.

2. On the Pictures toolbar, to alter the color contrast, click the **More Contrast** button , or the **Less Contrast** button . The graphic is updated in real time.

3. On the Pictures toolbar, to change the brightness, click the **More Brightness** button , or the **Less Brightness** button . The graphic is updated in real time.

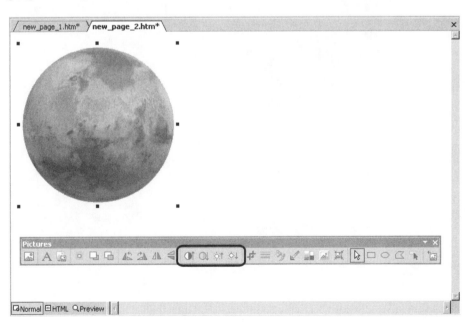

4. When you are satisfied with the settings for the graphic, click anywhere else in the document to deselect the graphic from further
editing.

Convert a Graphic to Grayscale

You can also convert a color graphic to grayscale. Grayscale applies black and
white shading values to color graphics, using a variety of gray tones in place of
the different colors.

1. In Page view, select the graphic you want to convert to grayscale.
Resize handles appear on the graphic and the Picture toolbar opens.

2. Click the **Color** button on the Pictures toolbar. A drop-down
menu opens.

3. Click **Grayscale**. The picture is now in black and white.

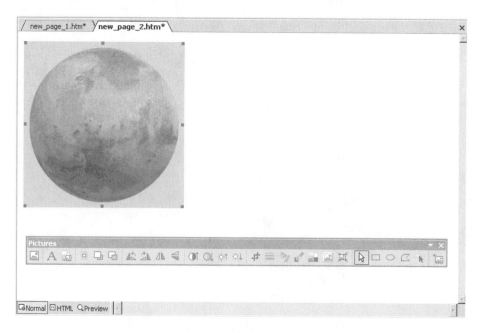

Wash Out the Color in a Graphic

You can introduce a wash, a gray art effect that increases the brightness but dims the contrast and serves as an excellent background.

1. In Page view, select the graphic you want to change. Resize handles appear on the graphic and the Picture toolbar opens.

2. Click the **Color** button 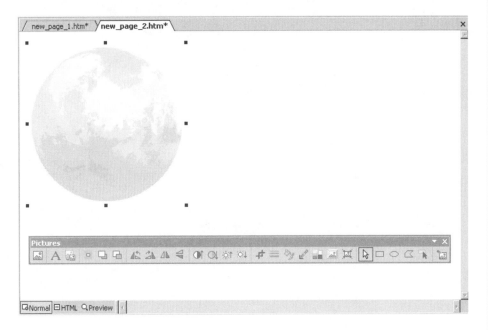 on the Pictures toolbar. A drop-down menu opens.

3. Click **Wash Out**. The picture has now been faded, or washed out.

Add Borders to a Graphic

It is also possible to add a one, two, three, or four-sided border. Special effects can be used to bevel the border or create the illusion of dimensionality.

1. In Page view, right-click the graphic you want to add a border, and then click **Picture Properties** on the shortcut menu. The Picture Properties dialog box opens.

2. Click the **Appearance** tab.

3. In the **Border thickness** box, enter a value for the width of the border in pixels. If necessary, experiment to get a sense of how the pixels work. To remove the border, type 0 (zero).

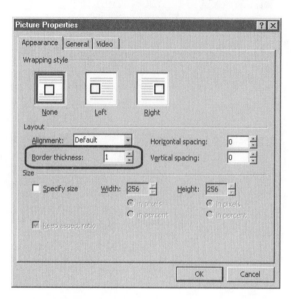

4. Click the **OK** button.

To introduce beveled borders, click the graphic, and then click the Bevel button on the Pictures toolbar. This transforms the edge of your graphic into a bevel-style frame. Continue to click the Bevel button until you are satisfied with the degree of the bevel. This beveled border can be eliminated by clicking Restore, the button at the right end of the Pictures toolbar. Remember, however, that this will restore all the changes you've made to this graphic since it was last saved.

When you set a default hyperlink for a graphic, FrontPage generates a border around the visual so that site visitors understand that they can click the graphic. If the graphic contains a default hyperlink, adding a border comprises the colors that you specified for hyperlinks.

Wrap Text Around a Graphic

You can wrap text around a graphic to attractively integrate text and graphics in a Web page. You can use the Wrapping Style options in the Pictures Properties dialog box to have text flow around the right or left side of a graphic.

1. In Page view, right-click the graphic you want to wrap around text, and click **Picture Properties** on the shortcut menu. The Picture Properties dialog box opens.

2. Click the **Appearance** tab.

3. In the **Wrapping Style** area, click the **Left** or **Right** box.

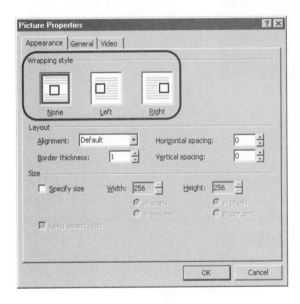

4. Click the **OK** button.

Make Colors in a Graphic Transparent

When a color is designated as transparent, whenever that color appears in the graphic, the background is visible through it. Graphics can have only one transparent color, and if you select a transparent color for a graphic that already has a transparent color selected, the original transparent color will revert to its original form. When you close the page, FrontPage prompts you to save the page in GIF format.

1. In Page view, select the graphic you want to change. Resize handles appear on the graphic and the Picture toolbar opens.

2. Click the **Set Transparent Color** button ✏ on the Pictures toolbar. When you move your cursor onto the graphic, it becomes an eye dropper.

3. Click the color within the graphic that you want to make transparent. Every pixel of that color is now rendered transparent, creating a speckling effect.

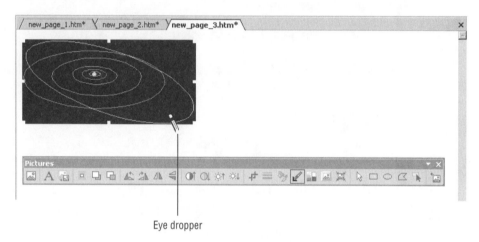

Eye dropper

Rotate and Flip Graphics

Rotating a graphic keeps the original front to back positioning and rotates the graphic clockwise or counter-clockwise to achieve the desired affect, while flipping a graphic creates a mirror graphic of a graphic, oriented either horizontally or vertically.

1. Select the Autoshape, Picture, Clip Art, or WordArt you want to flip or rotate.

2. To rotate the graphic, click either the **Rotate Right** button ↱ or the **Rotate Left** button ↰ on the Picture toolbar.

3. To flip the graphic, click either the **Flip Horizontal** button 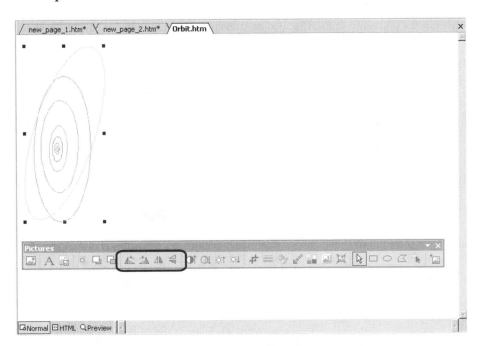 or the **Flip Vertical** button on the Picture toolbar.

Changing Graphic Properties

To change the properties of a graphic, you need to save the Web page on which the graphics appear. When you save the Web page, you will be prompted to save the graphics on that page, and you can set the format properties as JPEG, GIF, or PNG through the Save Embedded Files dialog box. This dialog box automatically opens any time you attempt to save a page containing a graphic element.

NOTE To change the properties of a JPEG, GIF, or PNG graphic that has already been saved to the page, you must modify the graphic somehow—such as rotating or cropping it—and then resave the page.

1. In Page view, display the Web page with the graphics you want to change.

2. Click the **Save** button 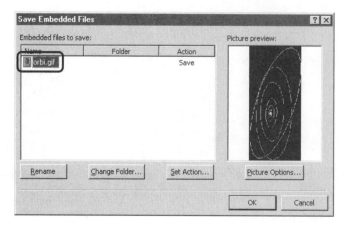 on the Standard toolbar to save the page with the graphic on which you want to change the properties. The Save Embedded Files dialog box opens.

3. In the **Embedded Files To Save** list, click the name of the graphic whose properties you want to reset.

4. Under the **Picture Preview** box, click **Picture Options**. The Picture Options dialog box opens. Perform either step 5 or step 6 below, depending on the format of the graphic.

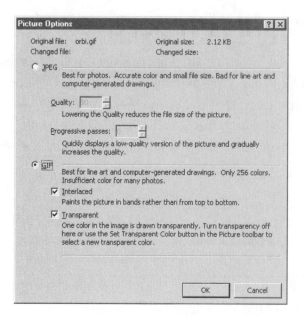

5. If the graphic is in JPEG format:

    a. In the **Quality** box, enter a quality value from 1 to 100, with 1 the lowest quality. Lowering the quality also reduces the file size.

    b. In the **Progressive Passes** box, enter a low quality value, which you can gradually enhance by moving the counter up one or two notches at a time and checking the results of each pass. This option produces a low-quality version of your graphic.

TIP   Not all web browsers support progressive passes.

6. If the graphic is in GIF format:

    a. Click the Interface check box to select or clear the option. An interlaced graphic loads in a series of bands, or strips, rather than from the top down.

    b. Click the Transparent check box to select or clear the option.

TIP   If the graphic is in PNG format, you can also change its properties, but this format isn't very common and isn't supported by all browsers.

7. Click the **OK** button to close the Picture Options dialog box.

8. Click the **OK** button.

Convert Graphic Formats

1. In Page view, right-click the graphic you want to convert, and click **Picture Properties** on the shortcut menu. The Picture Properties dialog box opens.

2. Click the **General** tab. In the Type area, the current type of the file, either GIF or JPEG is pre-selected.

3. Click the graphic conversion format (**GIF** or **JPEG**) option button you want to use.

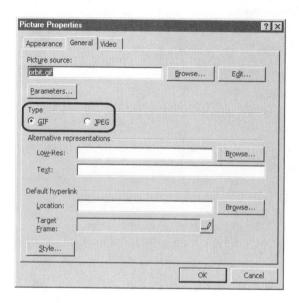

4. Click the **OK** button.

Changing the Way Graphics are Displayed

For a variety of reasons, the quality of the graphics you display on your Web site or page will have a major impact on the experience visitors have on your web. High quality graphics, for example, take much longer to load than lower resolution graphics, so you will lose some visitors before they even finish loading. Concurrently, very low quality graphics give a less than professional appearance to your web. Good designs strive for balance between these two considerations. For that reason, you will sometimes want to change the way graphics are displayed.

Configure a Graphics Editor Program

To create a low resolution version of a graphic by editing it in a third party graphics editor program, you must first configure the editor that you want to use in conjunction with graphic files. You only need to perform this operation once.

1. Choose **Tools** ➢ **Options**. The Options dialog box opens.

2. Click the **Configure Editors** tab.

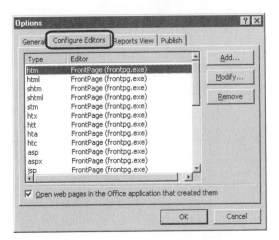

3. Click the **Add** button. The Add Editor Association box opens.

4. In the **File Type** box, type GIF.

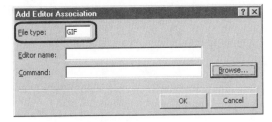

5. Click the **Browse** button, locate and select your graphics editor program, and then click the **Open** button.

6. Click the **OK** button. The file association is added to the list.

7. Click the **Add** button again. The Add Editor Association dialog box opens. In the **File Type** box, type JPG. Input the name of your graphics editor program, browse to locate the executable file for that program, and then click the **OK** button. The Add Editor Association dialog box closes and the file association is added to the list.

8. Click the **OK** button to close the Options dialog box.

Create Low Resolution Graphics

After you configure you graphic's editor program, you are ready to create a low resolution version of the graphic.

1. In the Page view, right-click the graphic you want to change, and then click **Edit Picture** on the shortcut menu. The graphic editor program opens.

2. Create a low resolution version of the graphic you want to use by following the instructions that are specific to the graphic editor program that you are using.

3. Returning to FrontPage, right-click the graphic to open the shortcut menu, and then click **Picture Properties**. The Picture Properties dialog box opens.

4. In the **Low-Res** box, enter the file name for the alternate low-resolution graphic you created, or click the **Browse** button to locate it.

> **TIP** Some Web browsers do not support low resolution graphics.

5. Double-click the graphic to associate it, and then click the **OK** button to close the Picture Properties dialog box and complete the process.

Adding Hyperlinks to Graphics

Graphics, like text, can contain hyperlinks. If you set a default hyperlink for a graphic, the web browser displays the hyperlink destination when the graphic is clicked.

> **TIP** For information on linking to external Web pages and e-mail addresses, see chapter 2.

Link to an Existing Internal Web Page

1. In Page view, right-click the graphic, then click **Hyperlink** on the shortcut menu. The Insert Hyperlink dialog box opens.

2. Under **Link To**, click **Existing File Or Web Page**.

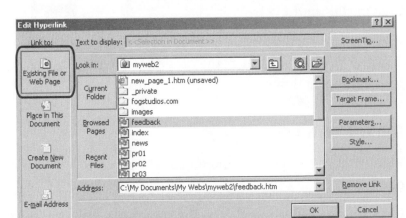

3. Browse to select the target page. The URL for the designated page appears in the address box.

4. Click the **OK** button to complete the link.

Link to a New Internal Page

1. In Page view, right-click the graphic, then click **Hyperlink** on the shortcut menu. The Insert Hyperlink dialog box opens.

2. Under **Link To**, click **Create New Document**.

3. In the **Name Of New Document** box, enter the name of the new document.

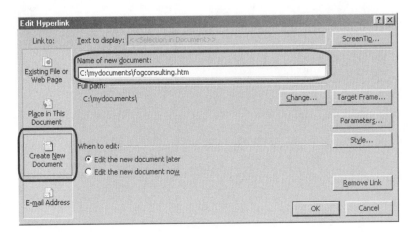

4. Click the **Edit The New Document Later** option button, and then click the **OK** button.

5. If you are prompted to save changes to your new blank document, click the **Yes** button, specify the destination to save the new file for later editing, and then click the **Save** button.

Link to a Bookmark

1. Right-click on the page containing the Bookmark. A shortcut menu opens.

2. Click **Hyperlink Properties** on the shortcut menu. The Insert Hyperlink dialog box opens.

3. Click the **Bookmark** button. The Select Place in Document dialog box opens.

4. Click the bookmark you want to use as the destination, and then click the **OK** button. You return to the Insert Hyperlink dialog box.

5. If you want the destination of the hyperlink to show up in a specific frame, click the **Target Frame** button. The Target Frame dialog box opens.

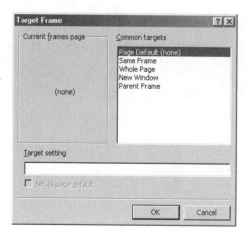

6. Specify the frame from the main window, and then click the **OK** button. The link is established.

Working with Graphic Hotspots

A hotspot is defined as an invisible region on a graphic, text block, or other web area to which you have assigned a hyperlink. A text hotspot is a word or a string of words that you have integrated into a graphic and that you have assigned to a hyperlink. When a site visitor clicks their cursor over that hyperlink, the link's destination is displayed in the Web browser. In FrontPage hotspots can be shaped as rectangles, circles, or polygons.

A graphic containing one or more hotspots is an Image map. Image maps typically provide cues so that you know where to click. You can also define a default hyperlink for a graphic rather than create a hotspot on it. When creating a button that is linked to your home page, for example, you can define a default hyperlink that leads to a specific destination, instead of drawing a hotspot around the entire button. The areas of the graphic that don't contain hotspots can be assigned a default hyperlink; when the user clicks anywhere outside a hotspot, they will be directed to the destination you set as the graphic's default hyperlink.

Add a Hotspot to a Graphic

1. In Page view, select the graphic you want to add a hotspot.

2. Click a hotspot button (**Rectangular**, **Circular**, or **Polygon**) on the Pictures toolbar that conforms to the shape you want.

3. Move the cursor over the picture until it becomes a drawing implement. Drag a hotspot. The shape you designated appears. You can size the hotspot by dragging the sizing handles. When you complete the hotspot, the Insert Hyperlink dialog box automatically opens.

4. Enter the URL you want the hotspot to link to, and then click the **OK** button. The hotspot is placed.

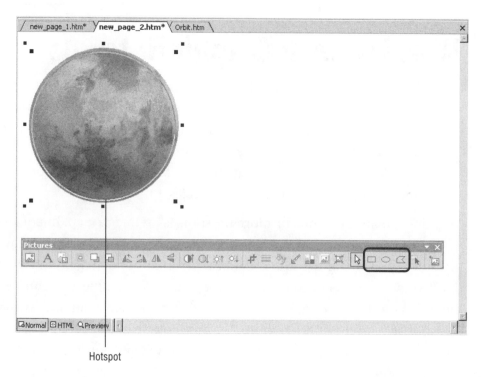

Hotspot

Add a Text-Based Hotspot

1. Select the graphic you want to add a text-based hotspot.

2. Click the **Text** button A on the Pictures toolbar. A text box appears in your graphic.

3. In the text field, type your text. To save your entry, click outside the graphic.

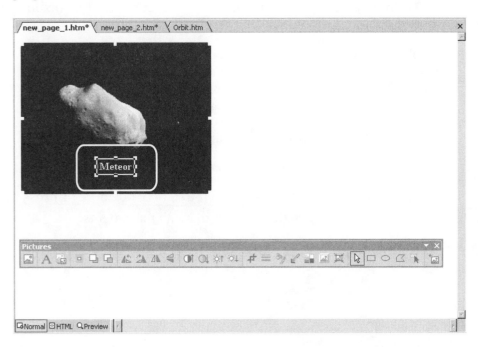

You can resize the text box by clicking and dragging the handles (the diagonal arrows in the corners of the box) or moving the text box by clicking and dragging a border (the double-headed, compass-style direction arrows in the middle of each side of the box).

4. Double-click an edge of the text box to open the Insert Hyperlink dialog box.

5. Enter the URL you want to link to.

All of the previous options for linking hotspots to existing web pages, internal or external, or to e-mail address are the same as those for linking entire graphics to these targets (see above for details).

6. Click the **OK** button to complete the link.

Edit Hotspot Hyperlinks

1. In Page view, select the graphics that contains the hotspot you want to modify.

2. Perform one or more of the following:

- ◇ Edit the URL for a hotspot—Double-click the hotspot, and alter the destination in the Address box.

- ◇ Resize the hotspot—Drag the selection handles.

- ◇ Delete a hotspot—Press the Delete key on the keyboard.

- ◇ Move the hotspot—Drag it to a new position, or press the arrow keys to move the hotspot in small increments.

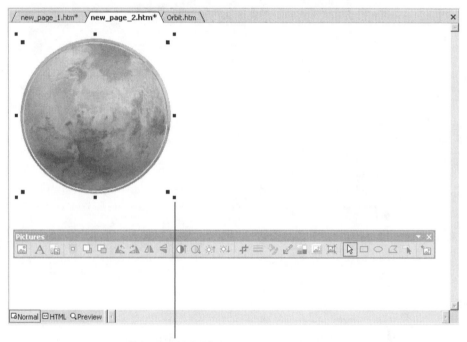

Hotspot resize handle

TIP   You can return a hotspot to its original position, if it is still selected, by pressing Esc.

5

Formatting Web Pages with Tables

In this chapter, you examine a feature that is invaluable to certain Web sites and pages. If your site is going to contain a lot of data, you will probably have occasion to use a table to tell the financial story, or to organize key information for your reader.

Creating Tables

Table

An orderly collection of information displayed within clearly-defined borders.

Cell

A single unit of a table, usually rectangle or square in shape.

Row

A series of horizontally-aligned cells within a table.

Column

A series of vertically-aligned cells within a table.

Though you might want to reference and analyze information, the best way to initially display large amounts of data is through the use of tables. **Tables** are defined by their various components; the **cell**, the **row**, and the **column**. The number of rows determines the height of the table, and the number of columns the width. The combination of the two determines the total number of cells that can hold information.

Here's the easiest way to create a table. Later in this chapter, you explore the many available variations.

Create a Table

1. In Page view, move the insertion point to the place on the page where you want the table to appear.

2. Choose **Table** ➢ **Insert** ➢ **Table**. The Insert Table dialog box opens.

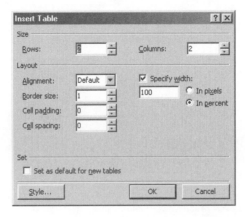

3. Define the attributes of the table by inputting values into the following fields:

◆ **Rows**—The number of rows you want in your table.

◆ **Columns**—The number of columns you want in your table.

◆ **Alignment**—The position you want to assign the text in the table (Flush Left, Flush Right, Centered, etc.).

◆ **Border Size**—The thickness level (measured in pixels) you want to assign to the table's border box. If you don't want a border, type 0 (zero).

- **Cell Padding**—The space, in pixels, between the data and the inside of the table cell.

- **Cell Spacing**—The space, in pixels, between the cells in a table.

- **Specify Width**—The width of the table in either pixels (insert the number of pixels) or percentages (insert the percentage of the available screen width you want the table to occupy).

> **TIP**
> If you like the settings you chose, click the Set As Default For New Tables check box to select it in the Insert Table dialog box. When you click the OK button, the new settings become the default values.

4. Click the **OK** button. A new table is inserted into your file.

2x2 table

Draw a Table

You can also create a table by drawing it, using the Draw Table feature of the Tables toolbar. You create the table by drawing each individual cell. This is useful when you want to create a custom table.

1. In Page view, display the page where you want the table to appear.

2. Choose **Table ➢ Draw Table**. The Tables toolbar opens with the Draw Table button  selected. When the Draw Table button is enabled, the cursor takes the shape of a pencil.

3. Position the pointer on the page you want to represent the upper left corner of the cell, and then drag the cell to make the desired dimension. When you have the desired shape, release the mouse button and the cell snaps into position.

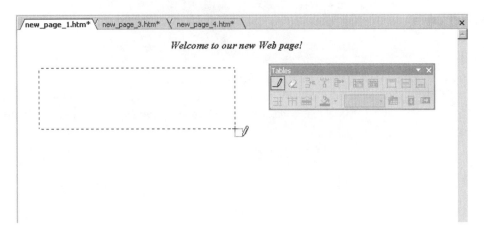

4. To divide the original cell into smaller cells, click the **Draw Table** button  on the Tables toolbar, and then draw a line

5. To remove a line, click the **Eraser** button on the Tables toolbar and move the cursor to your table. To erase a vertical or horizontal line, hold down the left mouse button and sweep the eraser icon across the line. As you cross the line, it briefly doubles, indicating that you are prepared to erase it. Release the mouse button and the line disappears.

TIP To resize a row or column quickly, position the pointer (which changes to the double-headed arrow) on the row or column border you want to resize, and then drag the border to the size you want.

6. When you're finished, click the **Draw Table** button on the Tables toolbar to deselect it.

Entering Text in a Table

Once you create your table you enter text into cells just as you would in a paragraph, except pressing the Tab key moves you from cell to cell. The first row in the table is good for column headings, whereas the leftmost column is good for row labels. To enter text in cells, you need to know how to move around the table and select the rows and columns.

WARNING Before you can select text in a table, the Draw Table button on the Tables toolbar needs to be deselect.

Enter Text and Move Around a Table

1. In Page view, position the insertion point in the table where you want to enter text. The insertion point shows where text you type will appear in a table.

2. Type your text, and then perform one of the following:

❖ Press the Enter key to start a new paragraph within that cell.

❖ Press the Tab key to move the insertion point to the next cell to the right (or to the first cell in the next row).

❖ Press the arrow keys or click in a cell to move the insertion point to a new location.

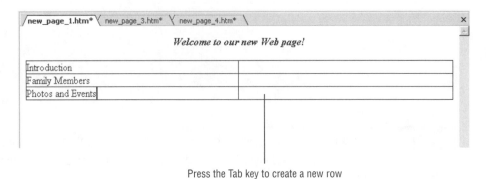

Press the Tab key to create a new row

Select Table Elements

Refer to the table for methods of selecting table elements, including the entire table, one or more rows and columns, and one or more cells.

To Select	Do This
The entire table	Click in a cell, and then choose Table ➢ Select ➢ Table.
One or more rows	Position the pointer along the left edge of the row you want to select (a black arrow appears), and then drag to select the rows you want, or choose Table ➢ Select ➢ Row.
One or more columns	Position the pointer along the top edge of the column you want to select (a black arrow appears), and then drag to select the columns you want, or choose Table ➢ Select ➢ Column.
A single cell	Drag a cell or click the cell with the black arrow, or choose Table ➢ Select ➢ Cell.
More than one cell	Drag with the black arrow to select a group of cells.

Adding Color to a Table

Tables are transparent by default, showing the background color or pattern of the web page as the background of the table. If this is not the best design choice, consider adding a different color as the background.

Add Color to Table Elements Quickly

1. In Page view, select the table, column, row, or cell you want to add color.

2. Click the **Fill Color** button drop-down arrow 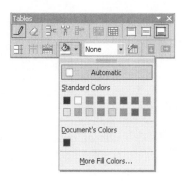 on the Tables toolbar. A menu opens.

3. Select a color on the menu.

> **NOTE** If you want to see more color choices, click More Colors, which opens the More Colors dialog box and offers a range of additional options.

Add Color to a Table Using Table Properties

1. In Page view, right-click on the table, and then click **Table Properties**. The Table Properties dialog box opens.

2. In the Background area, click the **Color** drop-down arrow 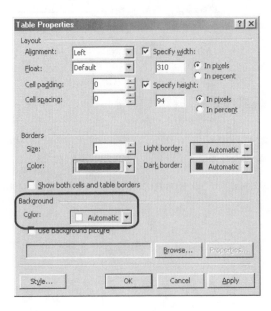, and then select a color.

3. Click the **Apply** button to insert the background color.

4. Click the **OK** button to close the Table Properties dialog box.

Formatting a Table

A uniform background color isn't always the best solution. For example, if you have a large table with a lot of columns, it might be easier for the reader to follow particular rows of information if your table uses alternating background colors for each row. Or perhaps you just want to have a different color in the first row or column (or both) to pull out the key terms that organize the data. Either way, you can use a color template to format your table, regardless of the number of cells it contains, or their arrangement.

Format a Table Quickly

1. In Page view, click the table to select it.

2. Choose **View** ➣ **Toolbars** ➣ **Tables**. The Table toolbar opens.

3. Click the **Table AutoFormat Combo** button drop-down arrow on the Tables toolbar. This produces a drop-down menu of format types.

If you are already familiar with these formats, select it directly from the menu. Otherwise, go directly to the next step

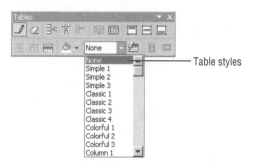

Table styles

4. Click the table format style you want.

Format a Table Using AutoFormat

1. Click the table to select it.

2. Choose **View** ➢ **Toolbars** ➢ **Tables**. The Table toolbar opens.

3. Click the **Table AutoFormat** button 📊 on the Tables toolbar. The Table AutoFormat dialog box opens, containing format styles, as well as a number of other options, including the ability to preview the various formats in thumbnail view.

4. Click a table style.

5. Click the format check boxes to select or clear additional formatting options.

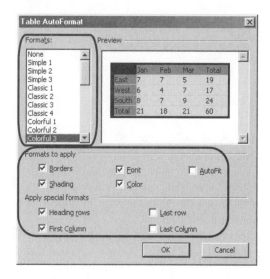

6. Click the **OK** button. The formatting is applied to your table.

Converting Text to a Table

Delimited text

Text in which each data field is separated by a comma, paragraph, or other character.

Text that has been **delimited** can be easily converted into a table.

Convert Delimited Text to a Table

1. In Page view, select the delimited text you want to convert to a table.

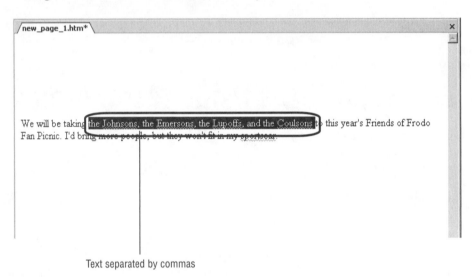

Text separated by commas

2. Choose **Table ➢ Convert ➢ Text To Table**. The Convert Text To Table dialog box opens.

3. Click the option button to designate the character used to separate the text (comma, paragraph, etc.).

> **NOTE** Clicking the None option button in the Convert Text To Table dialog box creates a one-celled table.

4. Click the **OK** button. The text is converted to a table.

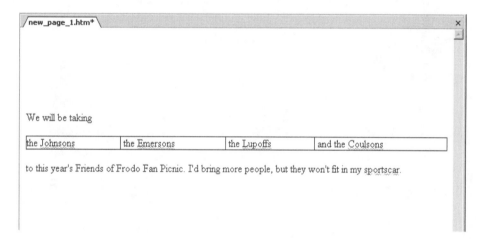

> **WARNING** HTML doesn't directly support tabs as a character to separate text, so we recommend avoiding them, if possible, despite their presence on the Convert Text to Table dialog box.

Adding Cells, Rows, or Columns to Tables

Suppose you have an existing table, and then decide to add another row or column of data. There is no need to recreate a larger table from scratch.

Add a Cell, Row, or Column to a Table

1. In Page view, click to position the insertion point to the right of the cell where you want to add another cell.

2. To add a single cell, choose **Table** ➢ **Insert** ➢ **Cell**. A new cell is added at the right end of the row containing the insertion point.

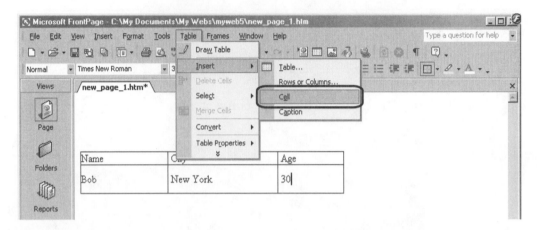

3. To add a row or column, choose **Table** ➢ **Insert** ➢ **Rows Or Columns**. The Insert Rows Or Columns dialog box opens.

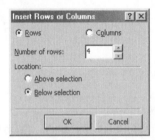

4. Enter the number of columns or rows you want to add to the table and, then click the **OK** button. The new columns or rows are added to the table underneath or to the right of the insertion point.

Splitting and Merging Cells

Cells can also be split or combined (also known as merged). Often there is more to modifying a table than adding or deleting rows or columns; you need to make cells just the right size to accommodate the text you are entering in the table. For example, a title in the first row of a table might be longer than the first cell in that row. To spread the title across the top of the table, you can merge (combine) the cells to form one long cell. Sometimes to indicate a division in a topic, you need to split (or divide) a cell into two.

Split a Cell into Two Cells

1. In Page view, right-click the cell you want to divide, producing a shortcut menu.

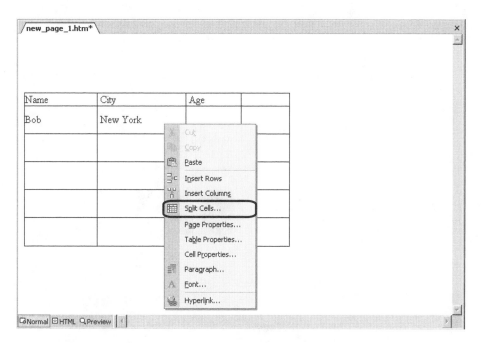

2. Click **Split Cells**. The Split Cells dialog box opens. Clicking the **Split Cells** button 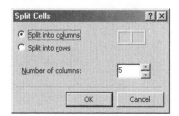 on the Tables toolbar also opens this dialog box.

3. Click the **Split Into Columns** option or **Split Into Rows** option button.

4. In the **Number Of Columns** or **Number Of Rows** box, type the number of columns or rows into which you want the cells split.

5. Click the **OK** button. The result appears in your table.

Merge Cells Together

1. In Page view, click a column, row, or group of adjacent cells and drag to select them. You can begin with two cells or select an entire group of adjacent cells.

2. Right-click a selected cell. This opens a shortcut menu.

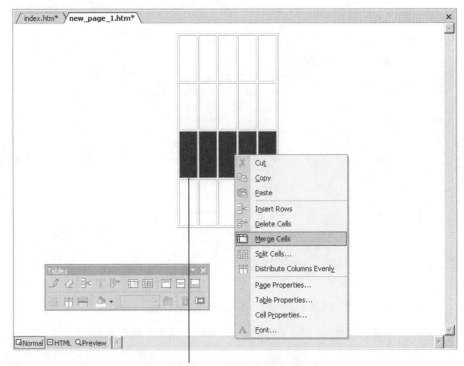

Selected cell in the table

3. Click **Merge Cells**. The cells merge into a single, larger cell.

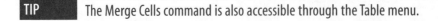

TIP The Merge Cells command is also accessible through the Table menu.

Creating Table Captions

Tables often require captions so the reader knows what he or she is looking at. Captions can be placed either at the top or bottom of the table.

Add a Caption to a Table

1. In Page view, place the insertion point anywhere inside the table.

2. Choose **Table** ➢ **Insert** ➢ **Caption**. The text insertion point appears at the top of the table (top is the default selection).

3. Type the caption for the table at the insertion point.

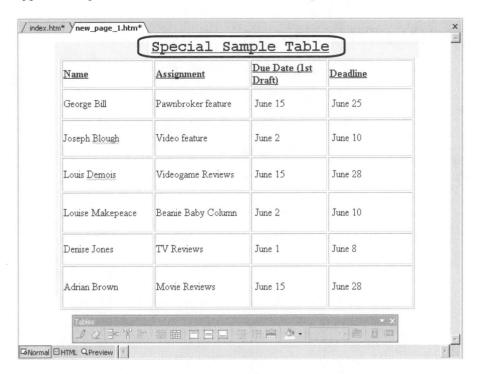

Change the Position of a Caption

1. In Page view, right-click the caption, and then click **Caption Properties** on the shortcut menu. The Caption Properties dialog box opens.

2. Click the **Bottom Of Table** option or **Top Of Table** option button.

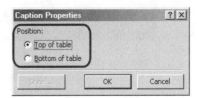

3. Click the **OK** button. The caption is repositioned.

TIP   To change the alignment of your table's caption, go to the Formatting toolbar and select Align Right, Align Left, or Center.

Deleting Table Elements

Tables, cells, rows, columns, and captions can all be easily deleted in Page view.

Delete a Table Element

1. In Page view, select the table, cell, row, column, or caption you want to delete.

2. Choose **Table** ➢ **Select**, and then:

- ❖ To delete a table, click **Table**.

- ❖ To delete a cell, click **Cell**.

- ❖ To delete a row, click **Row**.

- ❖ To delete a column, click **Column**.

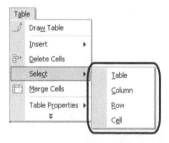

3. Choose **Table** ➢ **Delete Cells**.

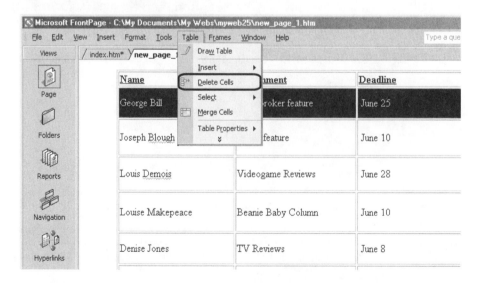

> **NOTE** To delete a table caption, highlight the caption and press Delete on the keyboard.

Filling a Table with Information

A table needs information, and while you will normally enter most of that data manually when creating a new table, text can also be easily copied into a row or column of cells.

Fill Cells with Information

1. In Page view, select that cell with the text to be copied along with the adjacent cells in a row or a column by dragging the cursor either to the right (row) or down (column).

2. Choose **Table** ➢ **Fill** ➢ **Right** or **Down**. All selected cells, in the row, or column now contain the text from the original cell.

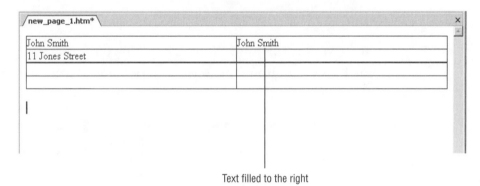

Text filled to the right

Adding Images to Tables

Because tables are supported by many browsers, they can be used to help lay out a page's text and graphics. It's also possible to define a background color or even a picture for either a single cell or an entire table.

Add an Image to a Table

1. In Page view, right-click the table or cell, and then click **Table Properties** on the shortcut menu. The Table Properties dialog box opens.

NOTE If you want to put the image inside a single cell instead of the entire table, click Cell Properties. The Cell Properties dialog box opens. The remainder of the steps mirror these for inserting an image as the background of a table.

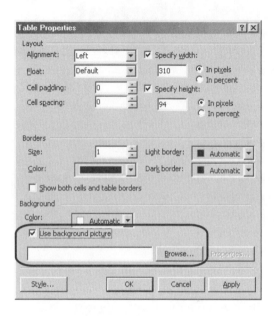

3. Click the **Use Background Picture** check box to select it, and then click the **Browse** button. The Select Background Picture dialog box opens.

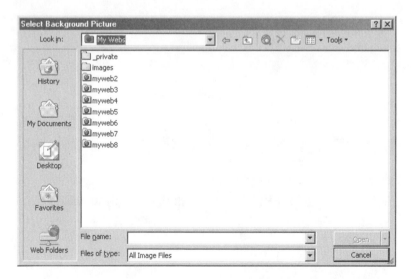

If the picture is on the World Wide Web, open your browser and display the Web page with the picture you want, right-click on the image, and then click Save Picture As. Use the Save Picture As box to save the file to your hard drive. Then switch back to FrontPage. The URL of the page you visited will be displayed in the File Name box. Click the OK button. The image is now displayed in your table or cell.

4. Click the **Look In** drop-down arrow, and then select the drive and folder where the picture is stored on a local drive or network.

5. Click the picture you want to use, and then click the **Open** button. The Table Properties dialog box appears.

6. Click the **OK** button. The picture is inserted in the table.

TIP Duplicating images—AutoShapes within tables, pictures, WordArt, or clip art—is easily accomplished. To make a single duplicate, select the image to be duplicated, and then choose File ➢ Copy. Then move the insertion point to the new location and click Paste. Continue to use the Paste command to generate multiple copies. Images from other Microsoft Office applications can also be copied using the Office Clipboard.

Changing Table Properties

Once you create a table and enter information, you can modify a variety of elements in the table, including alignment, cell spacing, cell padding (the space around the cell contents), height and width, border size, and color. You can change all of these properties in the Tables Properties dialog box.

Change Table Properties

1. In Page view, right-click the table, and then click **Table Properties**. The Table Properties dialog box opens.

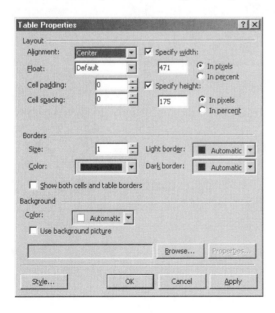

2. You can set the table's layout modifying the following parameters or accepting the default settings.

⬥ **Alignment**—Set the position for the table on the page (left, right, center)

⬥ **Float**—Indicate whether you want text surrounding the table to flow around the left or right side of the table. If you do not want text to flow around the table at all, select Default.

⬥ **Cell Spacing**—Change the space between the table cells by entering a number in the box.

⬥ **Cell Padding**—Change the space between a cell border and its content by entering a number in the box.

⬥ **Specify Width**—Set the width of the columns in pixels or percentage of the available screen space.

⬥ **Specify Height**—Set the height of the columns in pixels or percentage.

⬥ **Size**—Enter the width of your table border in pixels. If you don't want a border, enter 0 (zero).

⬥ **Color**—Select one color for the table border from the dialog box's drop-down color menu.

⬥ **Light Border** and **Dark Border**—Set a two-color border for a three-dimensional effect, select colors from the lists.

3. To show cell and table borders, click the **Show Both Cells And Table Borders** check box to select it.

4. To select a color for the table background, in the **Background** area, click the **Color** drop-down arrow ▾, and select a color from the Color palette.

5. Click the **OK** button. The various options have been applied.

Changing Cell Properties

You can use the Cell Properties dialog box to resize rows or columns of cells and change the span between cells in a table. You can also change the cell alignment, size, and border or background color.

Resize Cells, Rows, or Columns

1. In Page view, click to place the insertion point within a row or column you want to resize.

2. Choose **Table** ➢ **Select** ➢ **Row**, **Column**, or **Cell**.

3. Right-click the selected element, and then click **Cell Properties**. The Cell Properties dialog box opens.

4. To set the width, click the **Specify Width** check box to select it, and then enter a value in pixels or in percent.

5. To set the height, click the **Specify Height** check box to select it, and then enter a value in pixels or in percent.

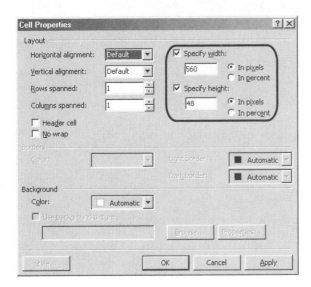

WARNING If the text or images are larger than the set values, the table or its elements will be upsized to contain the content.

6. Click the **OK** button. The cell, row, or column is resized.

Change Cell Span

The cell span feature is designed to create various widths or heights within cells on the same table. For example to set the span of a cell to two rows in height or two rows in width:

1. In Page view, right-click on the selected cell, and then click **Cell Properties** on the shortcut menu. The Cell Properties dialog box opens.

2. In the **Rows Spanned** and **Columns Spanned** boxes, enter 2 (two).

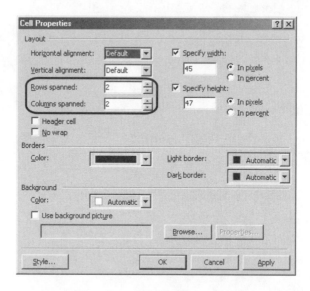

3. Click the **OK** button. The new format appears on screen.

Change Cell Layout

1. In Page view, select the cell whose properties you want to change.

2. Right-click the cell, and then click **Cell Properties** on the shortcut menu. The Cell Properties dialog box opens.

3. You can set the cell's layout using the following parameters:

◇ To set the horizontal alignment for the cell's contents, click the Horizontal Alignment drop-down arrow 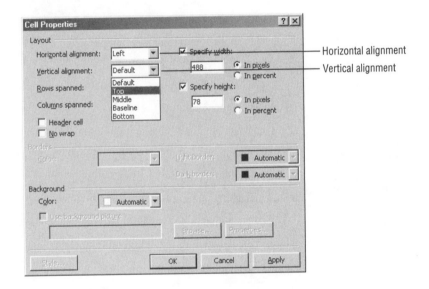, and then select an alignment.

◇ To set the vertical alignment for the cell's contents, click the Vertical Alignment drop-down arrow , and then select an alignment.

◇ To set cells as header cells, click the **Header Cell** check box to select it.

◇ To wrap your text within a cell, click the **No Wrap** check box to clear it.

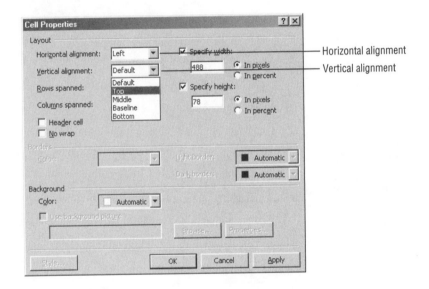

4. Click the **OK** button. Your selections are applied.

Change Cell Border or Background Color

A cell border can contain one or two colors (the second color adds depth, or a 3-D type), and each individual cell within a table can have its own one or two-colored border.

1. In Page view, right-click the table cell, and then click **Cell Properties** on the shortcut menu. The Cell Properties dialog box opens.

2. You can set the cell's border using the following parameters in the Borders area:

◇ To select a single-color border, click the **Color** drop-down arrow 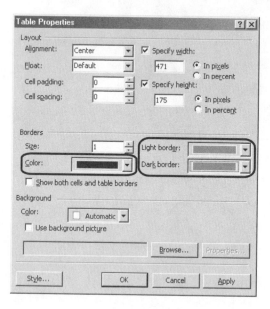, and then select a color.

◇ To select a two color border, and select a color from the **Light Border** drop-down arrow list and one from the **Dark Border** drop-down list.

3. You can set the cell's background using the following parameters in the Background area:

◇ Click the **Color** drop-down arrow, and then select a color.

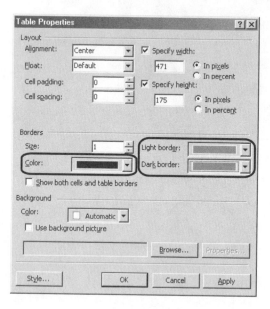

4. Click the **OK** button. Your selections are applied.

6 Creating Frames and Borders

● ●

A frames page is a type of HTML page that breaks up the browser display into different areas, known as **frames**. Each frame can display a different page. Pages are shown in frames by creating a hyperlink to the page and indicating the frame as a portion of the link. Frames are useful to Web masters because the user interface is stable and the frames contain built-in navigation. Frames pages are used for many different types of Web sites and pages, such as catalogs or sites containing a collection of articles.

Creating Frames Pages

Frames page
A form of HTML page containing no visible content that serves as a container that indicates which pages to display and where these pages should be displayed.

Shared borders
Areas of a page intended for content you want to appear on more than one of your Web pages.

Link bars
A collection of graphic or text buttons to hyperlinked pages both inside and outside your Web site.

Frames pages don't actually contain content; they are holders that indicate which content pages to display within the boundaries the frames page defines. For example, you can click a hyperlink within a frame, and have the linked page open in a different frame, called a target frame because it is the target of the link. Frames can also be split (vertically or horizontally), resized, or deleted by dragging frame borders. Frame borders can be seen or hidden by the user. You, as the webmaster, can determine the size of the margins inside each frame, the amount of space between frames, and whether a frame can be resized within a browser or if scroll bars should be included.

Frames pages can also contain **shared borders**—areas at the top, bottom, left, or right of a page—that are common to multiple pages in a Web site. Shared borders are used to include the same content on more than one page. Shared borders give your work a consistent appearance and often contain **link bars** to navigate to other frequently accessed pages within the site, or even to important pages external to the site.

Another advantage of shared borders is that you only need to edit content in one place to update all the pages that use the border. If, for example, some vital piece of information needs to be changed, change it on one page and the information is updated everywhere it appears within a shared border.

When you first work with borders you should use a frames page template, because templates are pre-configured so that you can easily move between frames. With a template, you decide what occupies the initial page (the page that is visible in each frame when you first visit a frames page), which can either be a new page or one you've previously created.

> **TIP**   If you add banners and link bars within a shared border, make sure you add the pages in Navigation view.

NOTE Remember that some of the content discussed in this section may not be applicable to every installation. It's a good idea, therefore, to see whether your browser supports frames before continuing your work in a frames page template.

Check for Frame Compatibility

1. Choose **Tools** ➢ **Page Options**. The Page Options dialog box opens.

2. Click the **Compatibility** tab. The Browsers List opens.

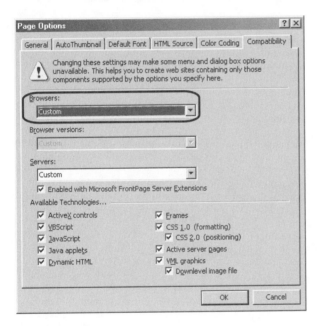

3. Click the **Browsers** drop-down arrow, and then select your browser. FrontPage will now display, under Available Technologies, which frames your browser supports.

The contents of the Browsers List are determined by your individual system configuration. Only browsers that you have previously installed appear on the list.

4. Click the **OK** button.

Create Frames Pages

1. In Page view, choose **File ➢ New ➢ Page Or Web**. The New Page Or Web task pane opens.

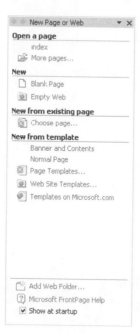

2. In the New Page or Web task pane under the New from Template heading, click **Page Templates**. The Page Templates dialog box opens, displaying the General tab.

3. Click the **Frames Pages** tab.

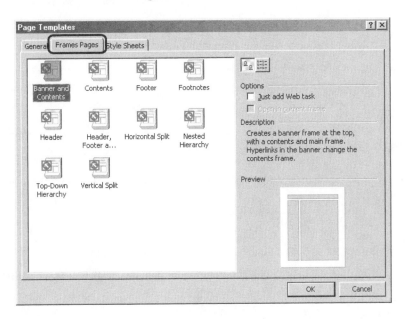

4. Select a template, and then click the **OK** button. The page opens in template form.

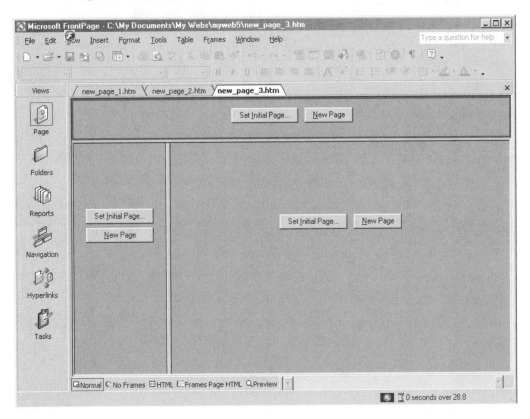

5. To create a new blank page in a frame, click the **New Page** button in the frame you've selected to house the initial page. FrontPage creates the new file, positions it in the frame, and establishes it as the initial page.

6. To insert an existing page in a frame, click the **Set Initial Page** button. The Insert Hyperlink dialog box opens. As the target of the hyperlink, you can select a page that you have previous created, one that you have visited recently, or create an entirely new page.

   a.   To select a page that you've created as the initial page, click the **Current Folder** button, select the page you want to open, and then click the **OK** button.

   b.   To select a page you have visited recently, click the **Browsed Pages** button, and then select the page from the list. Make sure the correct URL appears in the Address box, and then click the **OK** button.

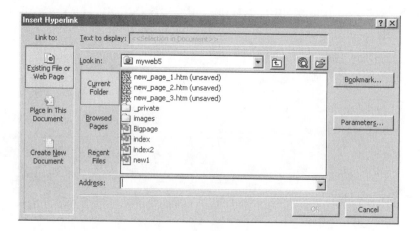

TIP   If you're using frames and frame pages for purposes of organization, avoid using shared borders or link bars, because they can create confusion among users.

Customizing an Existing Frames Page Template

You can modify an existing frames page template to create a customized template.

Customize an Existing Frames Page Template

1. In Page view, open a frames page template.

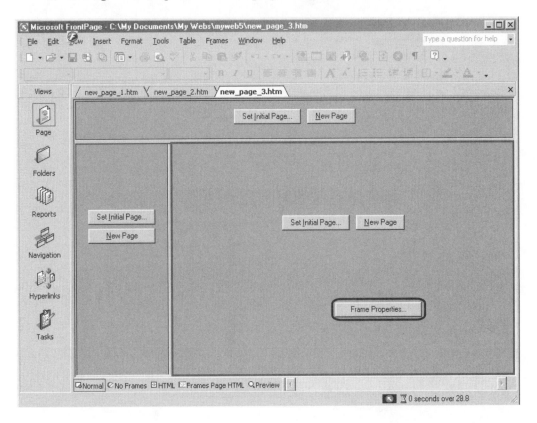

2. Click the **Frame Properties** button in a frame, or right-click in any frame, and then click the **Frame Properties** button. The Frame Properties dialog box opens.

3. Make any modifications to the size of the frame, margins, name and so forth that you desire, and then click the **OK** button.

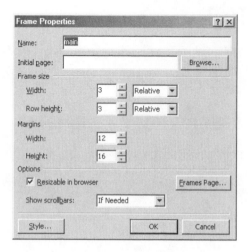

4. Choose **File ➢ Save As**. The Save As dialog box opens.

5. Click the **Save As Type** drop-down arrow , and then click **FrontPage Template**.

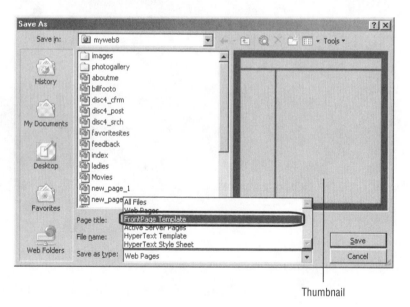

Thumbnail

6. In the **File Name** box, type the file name for your custom template.

7. Click the **Save** button. The Save As Template dialog box opens.

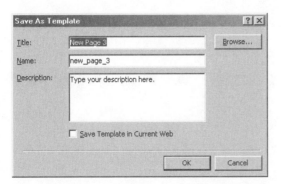

8. In the **Title** box, type the name you want to use as a title for the template. This is the title that will appear in the list of templates on the Frames Pages tab in the New dialog box.

9. In the **Description** box, type text describing what the template does. This text is displayed in the Description area of the Frames Pages tab.

10. Click the **OK** button.

> **TIP** If you've created a template and want it to be accessible to anyone working on the site, click the Save Template In Current Web check box to select it. FrontPage then creates a Shared Templates folder in the current site and adds your template to that folder.

Adding an Inline Frame

Inline frames resemble normal frames pages except an inline frame and its contents are embedded in an existing Web page. So you don't have to create a separate frames page to introduce embedded content. An **inline frame** can also create a frame within a frame. And anything you can do with a regular page can be done with an inline frame. Just as with any other frame, inline frames are customizable.

Inline Frame
A frames page with the contents embedded in an existing Web page.

Add an Inline Frame in a Web Page

1. In Page view, choose **Insert ➤ Inline Frame**. An inline frame appears on your page.

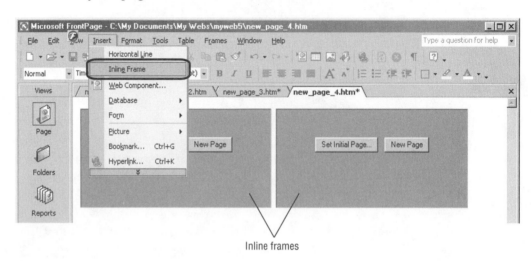

Inline frames

NOTE Each inline frame offers two option buttons: Set Initial Page or New Page. Using New Page you can create the contents of the frame from scratch.

2. Click the **Set Initial Page** button. The Insert Hyperlink dialog box opens.

3. Browse and locate the page you want to embed in the selected frame, and then click the page to be imported. The URL for the page appears in the **Address** box.

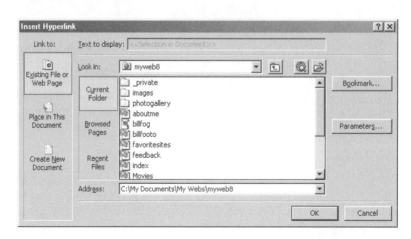

If you are working from a template or have inserted several inline frames, you can place new inline frames within existing frames by placing the insertion point in the desired frame, and then choose Insert ➤ Inline Frame. The inline frame appears in the designated spot.

4. Click the **OK** button. The selected page is now imported into the frame.

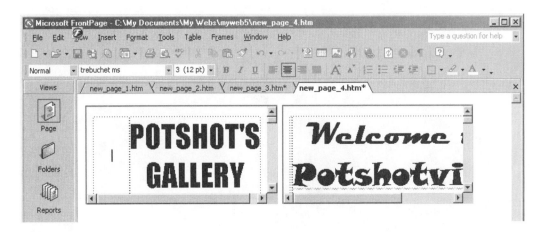

Using the Inline Frame command on the Insert menu, you can add multiple inline frames to your web page quickly.

Editing an Inline Frame

You can edit the properties of an inline frame at any time. You might want to do this to change the content page that it contains.

Change Inline Frame Properties

1. In Page view, select the inline frame you want to edit by moving your cursor to the frame's top border until the cursor changes into an arrow, and then right-click to open a shortcut menu.

2. Click **Inline Frame Properties**. The Inline Frame Properties dialog box opens.

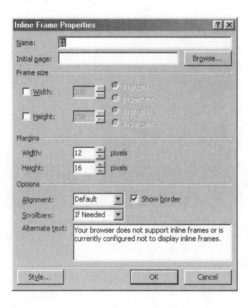

3. You can change the inline frame properties by modifying the following parameters or accepting the default settings.

◆ **Name**—The name of your inline frame.

◆ **Initial page**—The page that is first displayed in a frame when a visitor browses the site. This value enables you to set or edit the initial page within your inline frame.

◆ **Frame size**—The width and height of the frame in pixels or percentages.

◆ **Margins**—The margins of the frame in pixels.

◆ **Alignment**—The position for the inline frame on the page (left, right, or center)

◆ **Scrollbars**—When the scrollbars appear on screen. Set to Never Appear, Always Appear, or Appear If Needed.

◆ **Alternate text**—The text that you want the browser to display if the browser doesn't support frames.

◆ **Show border**—If you want a border drawn around the inline frame.

4. Click the **OK** button.

Saving a Frameset

After you've prepared your frames page, you need to save it. You are saving the frames page, or the **frameset.**

Save a Frameset

1. In Page view, open the frames page, and then click the Normal button.

2. Choose **File ➢ Save As**. The Save As dialog box opens, complete with a **thumbnail** showing the layout of the page. All of the affected elements are highlighted with a dark blue box so that you know which items are being saved.

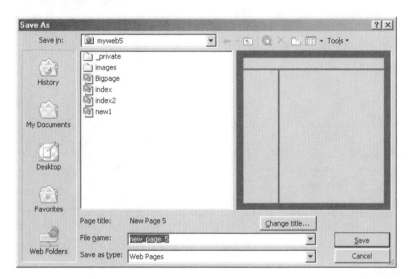

3. In the **File Name** box, type a file name for the highlighted frames page.

4. The page name can be changed by clicking **Change Title** in the dialog box. The Set Page Title dialog box opens. Type in the new title, and then click **OK** button.

5. Specify a location to save the Frameset, and then click the **Save** button. The Save As dialog box re-opens and requests that you save the page displayed in the frame you just saved.

6. Click the **Save** button.

Frameset

A page that breaks up a browser window into several modular areas, or frames that are capable of independently displaying multiple Web pages.

Thumbnail

A miniature depiction of a Web page graphic. It usually contains a hyperlink that leads to a larger version of the image.

> **NOTE** The title you see in the browser's title bar is the title of the frames page, not the title of the page displayed in that frame.

Save a Page within a Frameset

1. In Page view, open the frames page, and then click the **Normal** button.

2. Click the page or frame displaying the page you want to save.

3. Choose **Frames** ➤ **Save Page As**. The Save As dialog box opens.

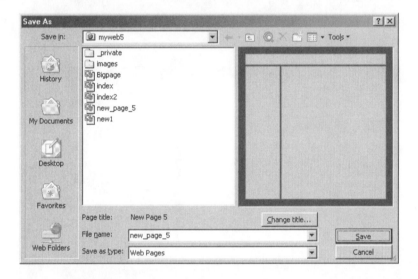

4. In the **File Name** box, enter (or choose) the file name for the page displayed in the thumbnail's selected frame.

5. In the **Save As Type** box, select the type of Web page you want saved.

6. To edit the page title, click the **Change Title** button. This opens the Set Page Title dialog box so that you can enter the new text.

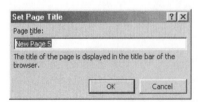

7. Specify a location where you want the page saved, and then click the **Save** button.

Splitting Frames

There are two ways to split a frame: by dragging its border, or by using the Slip Frame command on the Frames menu. When you split a frame, FrontPage creates a new frame and the content in the original frame remains intact.

Split a Frame Quickly

1. In Page view, click on the frame you want to split to select it.

2. Hold down the Ctrl key while you drag the frame border.

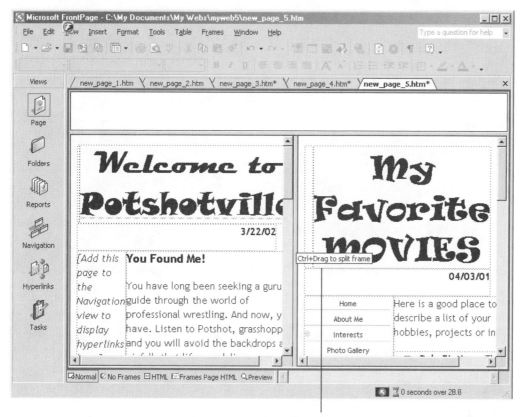

Frame border

Split Frames in Columns or Rows

1. In Page view, click on the frame you want to split to select it.

2. Choose **Frames** ➢ **Split Frame**. The Split Frame dialog box opens.

3. Click the **Split Into Columns** option button to split the frame vertically or click the **Split Into Rows** option button to divide the frame horizontally,

4. Click the **OK** button.

> **NOTE**   When you divide a frame, the content remains in the original frame while the new frame is created.

Deleting a Frame

When you no longer need a frame, you can delete it from a frames page. When the frame is deleted, the Web page in the frame is deleted, but the page is still available in your Web site folders. After you delete a frame, the remaining frames on the Web page expand to fill the space left by the frame you deleted.

Delete a Frame

1. In Page view, open the frames page, and then click the **Normal** button.

2. Click anywhere inside the frame you want to delete to select it.

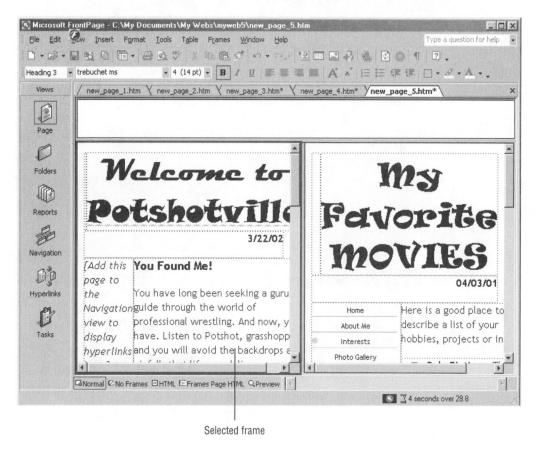

Selected frame

NOTE If the frames page contains only one frame, you cannot delete that frame.

3. Choose **Frames** ➢ **Delete Frame**.

Editing Frames Pages

Editing the content of a frame is another key in developing a solid site. When working in Page view, select the frame you want to edit by clicking it. The frame might be too small for you to work in easily. If this is the case, you'll want to open it in a larger window.

Open a Frame in a Window for Editing

1. In Page view, right-click anywhere in the frame. A dark blue border appears around the frame you're editing and a shortcut menu opens.

2. Click **Open Page In New Window**. The frame is now large enough to work in easily.

3. Choose **File** ➢ **Close** to return the page to its original size.

Display or Hide Borders Around Frames

You can display or hide borders around frames. When you display a border you can set the spacing between borders to achieve the look you want.

1. In Page view, right-click anywhere on the frames page.

2. Click the **Frame Properties** button. The Frame Properties dialog box opens.

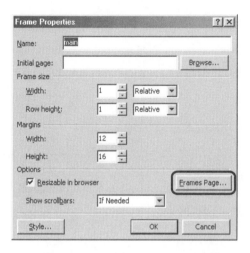

3. In the Options area, click the **Frames Page** button. The Page Properties dialog box opens, displaying the Frames tab.

4. Click the **Show Borders** check box to select or clear it. This affects all frames on your frames page.

5. If you select the Show Borders check box in the Page Properties dialog box, enter the amount of space, in pixels, you want between borders in the **Frames Spacing** box.

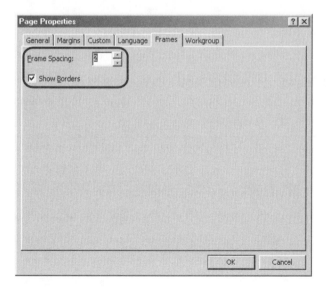

6. Click the **OK** button to close the Page Properties dialog box.

7. Click the **OK** button to close the Frame Properties dialog box.

Adjust Frame Margins

Frame margins set the distance between the frame content and the border.

1. In Page view, right-click in the frame, and then click **Frame Properties**. The Frame Properties dialog box opens.

2. In the **Frame Size** and **Margins** area, adjust the width and height settings.

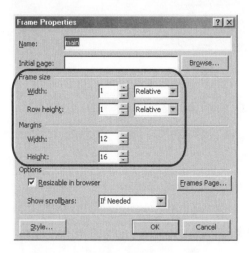

3. Click the **OK** button.

TIP To display or hide scroll bars, right-click in the frame, and then click Frame Properties. In the Frame Properties dialog box under Options, click the Show Scrollbars drop-down arrow, and then click If Needed, Never, or Always.

Edit the Target Frame

1. Select the text or graphic hyperlink, and then click the **Insert Hyperlink** button on the Standard toolbar. The Insert Hyperlink dialog box opens.

2. Click the **Target Frame** button. You now have two options.

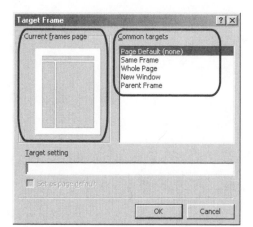

❖ In the Current Frames Page area, a map of your frames page is displayed. Click the frame you want to designate as the target frame.

❖ In the **Common Targets** box, click the target frame you want to designate as the target.

3. Click the **OK** button to close the Target Frame dialog box.

4. Click the **OK** button.

Working with Shared Borders

A shared border is a region on a Web page that is common to one or more pages in a Web site. A shared border is useful to place the same content, such as a logo, on multiple pages, rather than modifying each page. When you use shared borders, you only have to modify content in one place to update all pages.

Set Up Shared Borders

1. Open the Web site you want to set shared borders.

2. Choose **Format** ➢ **Shared Borders**. The Shared Borders dialog box opens.

3. Click the **Current Page** option or the **All Pages** option button.

4. Click the **Left**, **Right**, **Top**, and **Bottom** check boxes to select the borders you want to appear on this page.

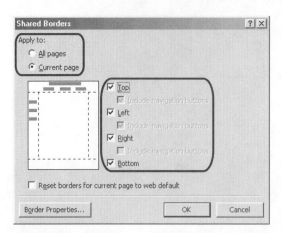

5. Click the **Border Properties** button. The Border Properties dialog box opens. Fine tune the selected borders, select a border position or a background color, and then click the **OK** button.

6. Click the **OK** button.

7

Inserting Multimedia and Special Effects

● ●

You have learned enough to begin thinking about the kind of features that are usually reserved exclusively for sites with unlimited budgets. The world of special effects, including multimedia inserts, is now available to even the most inexperienced Web designer through the tools available in FrontPage.

Changing Background Colors

Begin by adding background colors to your web page(s). When selecting background colors, some creative judgment is required. For example, if you choose a dark color for your background, make sure you use a light color for your text (The most commonly used is white) to generate the appropriate contrast required for easy reading.

NOTE Remember that you cannot place a background color on a page that is part of a theme. If you're working in a theme, the Background tab will not be available on the Page Properties dialog box. If you want to use a background color, click the Custom tab, select the theme listed under User Variables, and then click the Remove button. When you reopen the Page Properties dialog box, the Background tab is now available.

Change the Background Color

1. In Page view, right-click the page to which you want to change a background color, and then click **Page Properties** on the shortcut menu. The Page Properties dialog box opens.

2. Click the **Background** tab.

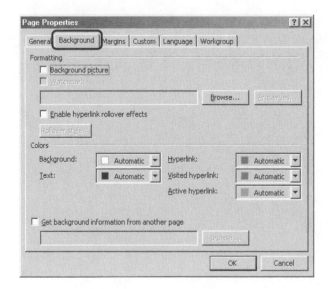

3. In the Colors area, click the **Background** drop-down arrow ![arrow]. A color palette opens.

4. Click the color you want on the color palette.

On the Background tab you also can select the color of the text, hyperlinks, visited hyperlinks, and active hyperlinks. These colors are selected in the same manner as the background color.

5. Click the **OK** button to close the Page Properties dialog box.

Access More Color Choices

If you don't like the available colors in the default palette, you can access a larger palette of choices.

1. In Page view, right-click an existing page, click **Page Properties**, and then click the **Background** tab. The Page Properties dialog box opens.

2. When you click any of the Colors options (background, text, hyperlink, visited hyperlink, or active hyperlink), a color palette opens.

3. Click **More Colors** on the color palette. The More Colors dialog box opens, containing a range of browser-safe colors. Then do one of the following:

❖ Click a color from the expanded palette. Every time you click a color, its corresponding hexadecimal value appears in the **Value** box. If you find a color you particularly like, make a note of its hexadecimal value for future reference.

❖ Enter a hexadecimal value in the **Value** box. An example of such a value would be HEX={99,FF,CC}. If you have recorded the value of a color that you liked previously, you can enter it directly here.

❖ Select a color from anywhere on the screen outside the More Colors dialog box. Click the **Select** button, and then click any color on the screen. Your cursor turns into an eye dropper as you move around the screen.

◇ Select a color that represents the color average of an area of the palette. Click the **Select** button, and then drag the eye dropper cursor to create a box encompassing the colors you want to average.

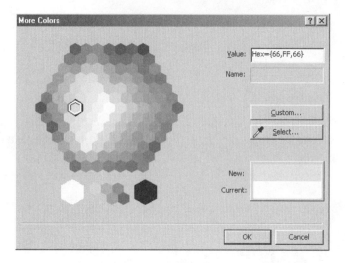

4. Click the **OK** button to close the More Color dialog box.

5. Click the **OK** button to close the Page Properties dialog box.

Define a Custom Color Palette

Even greater color selectivity is possible using the Colors dialog box to define a single shade, or even an entire custom palette.

1. In Page view, right-click an existing page, click **Page Properties**, and then click the **Background** tab. The Page Properties dialog box opens.

2. When you click any of the Colors options (background, text, hyperlink, visited hyperlink, or active hyperlink), a color palette opens.

3. Click **More Colors** on the color palette. The More Colors dialog box opens.

4. Click the **Custom** button. The Color dialog box opens.

5. In the Custom Colors area, click a blank box, then select a color by entering a combination of numerical values, or selecting one of the basic colors in the main palette or a custom color in the color spectrum palette.

NOTE   You can blend up to 16 different colors, and then save them to a custom palette.

6. Click the **Add To Custom Colors** button. The new color appears in the first custom colors box.

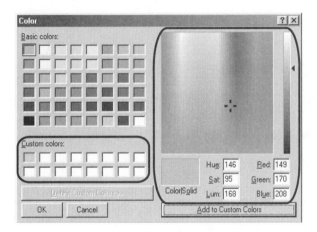

7. When you have completed defining custom colors, click the **OK** button to close the Color dialog box.

TIP   For special effects, click Custom and experiment with the sets of variables for Hue, Saturation, and Luminosity, or Red Green, and Blue.

8. Click the **OK** button again to close the More Colors dialog box. The selected custom background color appears in the Background box in the Page Properties dialog box.

9. Click the **OK** button to close the Page Properties dialog box and apply the custom color.

FrontPage displays color palettes appropriate for your page, such as:

- ❖ **Standard colors**—Basic 16-color palette.

- ❖ **Custom colors**—Palette containing colors you have defined.

- ❖ **Document's colors**—Colors being used on the current page.

- ❖ **Theme colors**—Colors used as part of the current theme.

- ❖ **More colors**—Palette used to define a custom color.

Inserting Background Pictures

You can also use a picture as the background for a page. Pictures can be taken from elsewhere on your site, a file, clip art, or the World Wide Web. You can also use a background picture in **watermark** form, a graphic that doesn't scroll along with the page.

NOTE   Not all Web browsers support watermarks.

Insert a Background Picture

1. In Page view, right-click anywhere on the page to which you want to insert a background picture, and then click **Page Properties** on the shortcut menu. The Page Properties dialog box opens.

2. Click the **Background** tab.

3. In the Formatting area, click the **Background Picture** check box to select it. When this option is selected, the Watermark option becomes active. If you want to create a watermark, click the **Watermark** check box to select it.

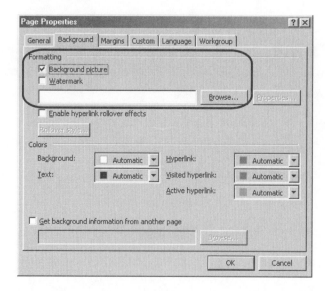

4. Click the **Browse** button. The Select Background Picture dialog box opens.

Watermark

A graphic that appears in the background of a Web page, but does not scroll as the page scrolls.

5. Click the **Look In** drop-down arrow, and then select the folder location (hard drive-based or network-based) containing the picture you want to use.

NOTE

> **NOTE** If the picture originates on the Web, click Search the Web, browse to find the picture you want, then toggle back to FrontPage. The URL is displayed in the File Name box.

6. Select the picture you want to insert, and then click the **Open** button. The picture you selected now opens as a background image. The Page Properties dialog box appears, displaying the file name and location.

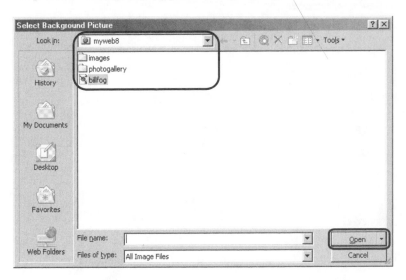

7. Click the **OK** button. The picture appears as the background for the page.

Adding Special Effects to Text

FrontPage comes with simple special effects you can quickly add to text on your Web pages. Some of the effects add style to your text, such as Blink or Overline, while others define the type of text, such as Definition or Citation, on your Web pages.

Add Font Effects to Text

1. In Page view, select the text you want to format.

2. Choose **Format ➤ Font**. The Font dialog box opens.

3. In the **Effects** area, click any of the font effects check boxes to select or clear them.

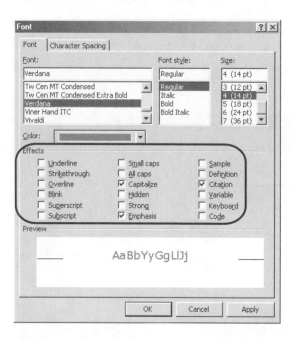

The font effects unique to FrontPage include:

◊ **Overline**—Draws a line above the text.

◊ **Blink**—Applies blinking animation to the text.

◊ **Capitalize**—Capitalizes the first letter in each word.

◊ **Hidden**—Makes the font invisible.

◊ **Strong**—Applies a stronger emphasis to the text (for example, bold).

◊ **Emphasis**—Applies a subtle emphasis to the text (for example, italic).

◊ **Sample**—Applies a fixed width font to the text.

◊ **Definition**—Specifies the text as a definition.

◇ **Citation**—Specifies the text as a citation or reference to other sources.

◇ **Variable**—Specifies the text as a variable or program argument.

◇ **Keyboard**—Specifies the text that is entered by a user.

◇ **Code**—Specifies the text as programming code.

4. Click the **OK** button. The text is formatted to your specifications.

Changing the Color to Links

When you use text as a hyperlink, you want to make sure that the link is colored differently from the rest of the text, also that the link changes color after a user has visited it as this is a common convention on the Web.

Change the Color to Links

1. In Page view, right-click an existing page, and then click **Page Properties** on the shortcut menu. The Page Properties dialog box opens.

2. Click the **Background** tab.

3. Select the link colors you want using the **Hyperlink**, **Visited Hyperlink**, and **Active Hyperlink** drop-down arrows .

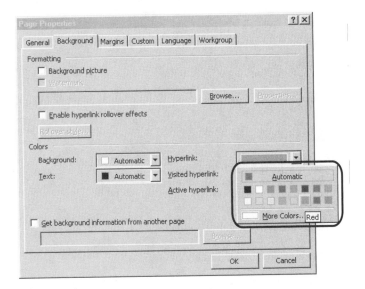

4. Click the **OK** button.

This is a sample web page and it links to several other sites, including one of films, music, television, and professional wrestling.

Link with color changes

You can add special effects to hyperlinked text that causes the font to change when a visitor passes their cursor over it. Right-click the hyperlinked text, click Page Properties, and then click the Background tab. In the Formatting area of the Page Properties dialog box, click the Enable Hyperlink Rollover Effects check box to select it. Click the Rollover Style button. In the Font dialog box, set the rollover properties for hyperlinks on the current page, and then click the OK button. Hyperlink rollovers are not supported by all browsers.

Creating a Photo Gallery

They say a picture is worth a thousand words, but a good caption helps readers to get all the nuances of a picture immediately. Also, for readers who disable graphic downloads in their browsers, a caption is one of the only options you have of conveying to them the intent of the illustration.

NOTE   Text boxes for a Caption or Description are not available in the Montage Layout.

Create a Photo Gallery

1. In Page view, position the insertion point at the spot on an existing page where you intend to add a photo gallery or click **Blank Page** in the **New Page Or Web** task pane.

2. Choose **Insert ➢ Web Component**. The Insert Web Component dialog box opens.

3. In the left pane, click **Photo Gallery**. Photo Gallery options appear in the right pane.

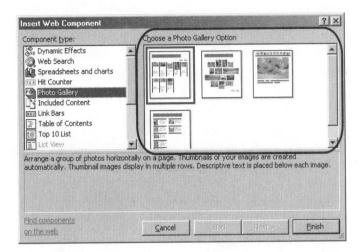

4. In the right pane, select the layout you prefer for your photo gallery. Select a layout thumbnail and a description of that layout opens in the text area below the layout samples.

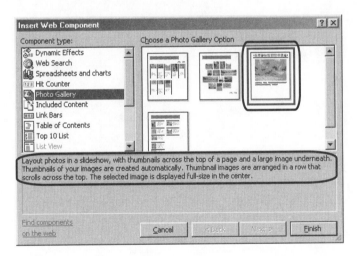

5. Click the **Finish** button. The Photo Gallery Properties dialog box opens.

6. Click the **Add** button. The Add menu opens, displaying two commands, **Pictures From Files** and **Pictures From Scanner Or Cameras**, you can use to insert a graphic into the photo gallery.

◊ To select a picture from a file, click **Pictures From Files**. A selection of available files opens. Select the graphic you want, and click the **Open** button.

◆ To select a picture from a scanner or digital camera, first select **Pictures From Scanner Or Cameras** and make sure that the device (camera or scanner) that contains the picture is connected to your computer. Set the resolution (the higher the resolution, the higher the image quality, and the longer it will take to load when someone visits your web), select either **Insert** or **Custom Insert**, depending on the input device, and then follow the prompts.

TIP You can use the Add button in the Photo Gallery Properties dialog box to insert multiple graphics at the same time.

7. To arrange the pictures within your gallery, select the name of the graphic, and then click the **Move Up** button or the **Move Down** button.

8. To set the width and the height of the thumbnail, enter width and height values in the **Width** and **Height** boxes.

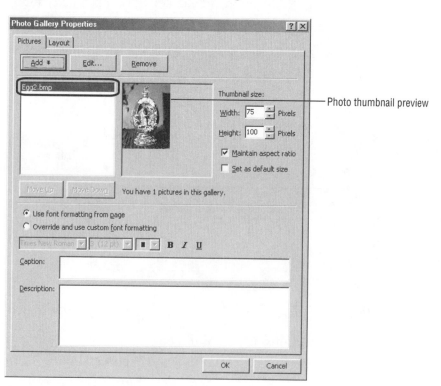

Photo thumbnail preview

TIP To rotate, crop, and change the size of a picture in the photo gallery, click the Edit button in the Photo Gallery Properties dialog box.

9. Click the **OK** button.

Add a Caption to a Picture in the Photo Gallery

1. In Page view, right-click the photo gallery in which you want to add captions, and then click **Photo Gallery Properties** on the shortcut menu. The Photo Gallery Properties dialog box opens.

2. Select the picture in which you want to add a caption. A preview of the picture opens next to its name.

3. In the **Caption** box, type the caption that you want to appear with the picture. The caption is always visible.

4. In the **Description** box, enter the text you want to appear when a user passes their mouse over the picture. Descriptions appear in pop-up ScreenTip boxes, and are used to provide additional detail about a picture.

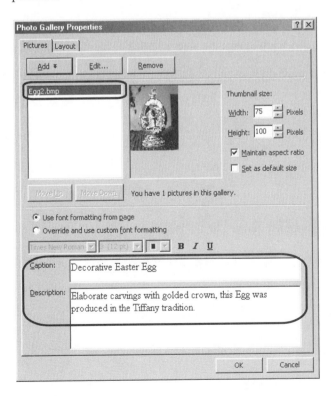

5. Click the **Layout** tab.

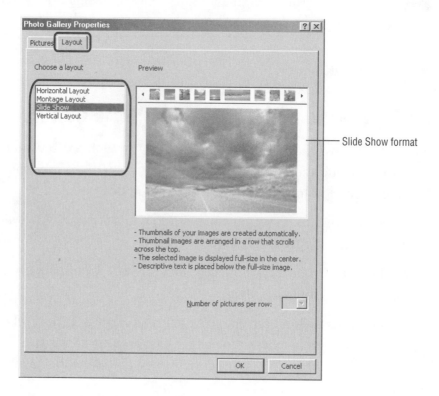

Slide Show format

6. Choose one of the layouts.

7. In the **Number Of Pictures Per Row** box, enter a value for the number of pictures that you want in a row.

> **NOTE** In Slide Show and Montage layouts, the seventh step is not available.

8. Click the **OK** button.

Adding Background Sound

You can introduce background sounds to accompany and enhance your web. There's nothing like hearing a favorite tune when you enter a site or visit a particular page. The sound can be played continuously in a loop, or you can set it for a desired number of plays.

Not all Web browsers support background sound.

Add a Background Sound to a Web Page

1. In Page view, right-click the page to which you want to add a background sound, and then click **Page Properties** on the shortcut menu. The Page Properties dialog box opens.

2. Click the **General** tab, if necessary.

3. In the **Location** box, type the sound file name or click the **Browse** button, locate and select the sound file you want to use, and then click the **Open** button.

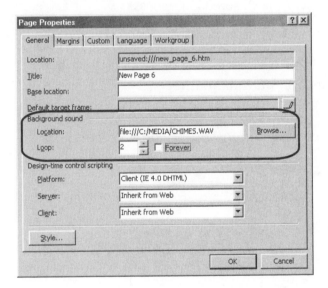

4. To set the sound to repeat continuously, click the **Forever** check box to clear it, and then click the number arrows in the **Loop** box to set the number of times you want the sound to play.

5. Click the **OK** button. Hereafter, whenever a visitor opens the page, they will hear the sound effect you chose.

Adding Sound Effects Using Hover Buttons

Hover button

A button that a site visitor can click to link to a page, sound, graphic, or other Web element.

Beyond simple sound bites that run automatically when a user enters a page, you can also tie sound effects and music to Web elements so that they play when a user performs an action. To do so, you must create a **hover button** that users can click to produce a pre-set sound effect or other audio playback.

Create a Hover Button

1. In Page view, position your insertion point at the location where you want to insert the hover button, and then click the **Normal** tab in the lower left corner of your screen, if necessary.

2. Choose **Insert** ➢ **Web Component**. The Insert Web Component dialog box opens.

3. In the left pane, click **Dynamic Effects**.

4. In the right pane, click **Hover Button**, and then click the **Finish** button. The Hover Button Properties dialog box opens.

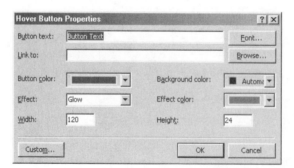

5. In the **Button Text** box, type the hover button's text label. (If you intend to use a custom picture for the button that already has a text label, clear the default value).

6. In the **Link To** box, type the URL of the sound file you want to play when the hover button is clicked, or click the **Browse** button to locate the file.

Hover buttons can also be used to call up multimedia video files, graphics, and so forth in addition to sound files.

7. Click the **Custom** button. The Custom dialog box opens.

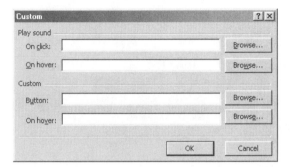

Hover buttons are, in fact, Java applets, so only the .au format (.au files in 8-bit, 8000 Hz, mono, u-law format to be precise) will work with hover buttons. Sorry, no .wav or .midi files.

8. If you want the sound to play when a visitor clicks it, enter the sound's URL (or locate it using the Browse button) in the **On Click** box. If you want the sound to play when the visitor's cursor is over the button, place the same information in the **On Hover** box, and then click the **OK** button to close the Custom dialog box.

9. Click the **OK** button and the hover button appears on the page.

Don't forget to use the Preview feature so that you can see how the hover button looks in a browser.

Inserting Video Clips

Streaming video clips are becoming more accessible to a broader base of users as high speed internet access using cable modems, DSL and other technologies become more prevalent. FrontPage can insert pre-recorded video clips into your Web pages using the Insert menu.

| NOTE | As with other features in FrontPage, not all browsers support video. |

Insert a Video Clip

1. In Page view, position the insertion point at the location where you want to insert your video.

2. Choose **Insert** ➢ **Picture** ➢ **Video**. The Video dialog box opens.

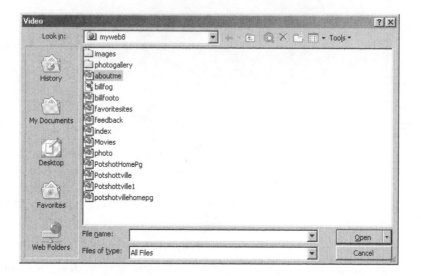

3. Click the **Look In** drop-down arrow ▼, and then select the folder location (hard drive-based or network-based) containing the video you want to use.

4. Select the video file, and then click the **Open** button. The video appears on your Web page.

Change Video Clip Properties

1. In Page view, right-click the video clip, and then click **Picture Priorities** on the shortcut menu. The Picture Properties dialog box opens.

2. Click the **Video** tab, and then select the options you want.

   ◆ **Forever** check box—runs the video continuously.

   ◆ **Loop** box—sets the number of times you want the video to play. This option is only available when you clear the **Forever** check box.

◇ **Loop Delay** box—sets a slight delay before each replay of the video. Enter the delay time in milliseconds in the Loop Delay box.

◇ **On File Open** option—runs the video whenever its page is loaded into a browser.

◇ **On Mouse Over** option—runs the video whenever a visitor moves their cursor over the video hover button.

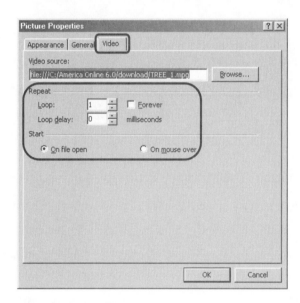

3. Click the **OK** button.

Creating Marquees

A **marquee** is an especially attractive visual special effect. Much as a movie theater marquee shows off what film is playing, a Web marquee helps your Web site stand out.

Create a Marquee

1. In Page view, select the position you want to place the marquee, or select the existing text that you want to display inside the marquee.

2. Choose **Insert ➢ Web Component**. The Insert Web Component dialog box opens.

Marquee
An animated banner commonly used in headers to draw attention to the title of the site.

3. In the left pane, click **Dynamic Effects**, and then click **Marquee** in the right pane.

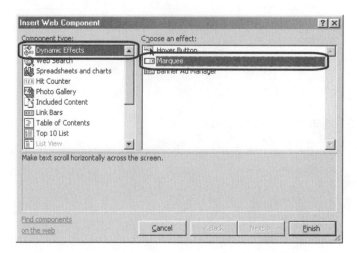

4. Click the **Finish** button. The Marquee Properties dialog box opens.

5. Set the values for marquee speed and select options for the marquee direction and behavior.

6. Click the **OK** button. A non-animated version of the marquee appears on the page.

7. To get an idea of how this page will look online, click the **Preview** tab in the lower left corner of your screen and you'll see the animations, scrolling, and other features that you selected.

Customize a Marquee

1. In Page view, right-click the marquee you want to edit, and then click **Marquee Properties**. The Marquee Properties dialog box opens.

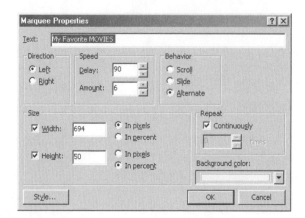

2. Modify these properties to suit the effect you are trying to achieve.

◆ **Text**—Text you want to display inside the marquee. There is no limit on length.

◆ **Direction**—Determines whether your text within the marquee moves left or right.

◆ **Speed**—How fast the text in a marquee moves.

◆ **Delay**—Length of the delay, in milliseconds, before the marquee text begins to move.

◆ **Amount**—The increment, in pixels, that the text in the marquee moves.

◆ **Behavior**

Scroll—Text scrolls horizontally across the screen.

Slide—Text slides into view.

Alternate—Text alternates between scrolling and sliding.

◆ **Size**—Select the Width or Height check box, and then type the width or height. Next, select whether the width and height are being measured in pixels or as a percentage of the browser window.

◆ **Continuously**—Determines how many times the text effect in a marquee is repeated.

To repeat the marquee continuously, select the **Continuously** check box.

To repeat the marquee a fixed number of times, clear the **Continuously** check box, and then type the number of times the marquee should be repeated.

◆ **Background Color**—Specifies the color you want displayed behind the marquee's scrolling text.

3. Click the **OK** button to save your settings.

TIP To expand or contract the spacing between characters, or to raise or lower the text, click the Style button in the Marquee Properties dialog box. The Modify Style dialog box opens. Click the Format button, and then click Font on the shortcut menu. The Font dialog box opens. Click the Character Spacing tab, make the changes you want, and then click the OK button twice to go back to the Marquee Properties dialog box.

Inserting a Dynamic HTML Effect

You can add special effects to your Web pages by using **Dynamic HTML (DHTML).** With DHTML, you can animation text to fly off the page one word at a time or change a long list of points into a space-saving collapsible outline. An animation effect is tied to a trigger event on the part of the visitor. The trigger event can be anything from clicking a link to entering the site.

Insert a Dynamic HTML Effect

1. In Page view, select the item you want to animate, and then choose **Format ➤ Dynamic HTML Effects**. The DHTML Effects toolbar opens.

2. Click the **On** down arrow  on the DHTML Effects toolbar, and then select the event (such as **Click**, **Double Click**, **Mouse Over**, and **Page Load**) that will trigger the animation. The events listed in the On box are determined by the type of page effect you select.

Completed DHTML Effects toolbar

3. Click the **Apply** down arrow ▪ on the DHTML Effects toolbar, and then select the kind of animation effect you want. As with the On box, the options are determined by the kind of page element you selected and the type of On event you selected. The main effects include: (Fly Out, Fly In, Drop In By Word, Elastic, Hop, Spiral, Wave, Wipe and Zoom). Other effects include:

◇ **Formatting**—Generates an animation that changes the look of a page elements, such as a font changing color.

◇ **Swap Picture**—Generates an animation that exchanges pictures.

◇ In the **Choose Settings** box, click the down arrow ▪, and then select the settings for the effect.

4. Click the **Effect** down arrow ▪ on the DHTML Effects toolbar, and then click a Formatting effects. From this menu, you can select the font style, size, color, effects, and character spacing.

5. After you've selected an animation in the **Apply** or **Effects** boxes, you will be given automatic access to a series of options. The settings are:

◇ Choose **Font** (If you assigned a Formatting Animation, you can change the font style, size, color, effects, and character spacing).

◇ Choose **Border** (If you assigned a Formatting Animation, this changes the border or shading).

◇ Choose **Picture** (If you selected a picture and initiated the Swap Picture feature, select this to select the picture you want to swap with the existing picture.)

> **TIP** To remove the DHMTL effect, click the Remove Effect button on the DHTML Effects toolbar.

> **TIP** To highlight the area with the DHTML effect, click the Highlight Dynamic HTML Effects button on the DHTML Effects toolbar.

6. When you're done setting the effects, choose **Format ➤ Dynamic HTML Effects** to close the DHTML Effects toolbar.

Inserting Browser Editable Lists

If you are collaborating with a group in a Web based environment, and your server is running Microsoft SharePoint team services, you can create and display various types of interactive lists, Web elements that store and display data that users can edit on the Web through their browsers.

To Create a Custom List:

1. Choose **File ➢ New ➢ List**. The List dialog box opens.

2. Double-click **New List Wizard**. The wizard opens.

3. When the first wizard screen opens, click the **Next** button.

4. In the **Name** box, type a name from the list, add a description in the **Description** box, then click the **Next** button.

5. Click the **Add** button. The Field Name dialog box opens.

6. In the **Field Name** box, enter a designation for the field and add a description in the **Description** box.

7. In the **Information Type** list, enter the type of data you want to store in this field.

8. Click the **Next** button.

9. When you have all the settings the way you want them, click the **Finish** button.

10. Repeat steps four through eight for each new box you want to add.

11. Click the **Next** button.

12. Set the list's permission settings (for Web site visitors who have total access to your site).

13. Click the **Finish** button.

8 Drawing and Modifying Objects

When you need to add pictures to a spread-sheet, Microsoft FrontPage 2002 is all you need to get the job done. You can choose from a set of pre-designed shapes, or you can use tools that allow you to draw and edit your own shapes and forms. FrontPage's drawing tools control how you place objects on your worksheet in relation to one another. If you choose to combine objects, you can create sophisticated effects.

Drawing Objects

Lines
Straight or curved lines (arcs) that connect two points.

Drawing objects can be classified into three categories: lines, AutoShapes, and freeforms. **Lines** connect two points, **AutoShapes** are preset objects, such as stars, circles, or block arrows, and if you want to construct a new shape, you can draw a **freeform** shape.

AutoShapes
Preset objects, such as arrows, common shapes, banners, circles, or callouts.

Once you have created a drawing object, you can manipulate it in many ways, such as rotating it, coloring it, or changing its style. Excel also provides formatting commands that afford you precise control over your drawing object's appearance.

Freeform
A drawing with irregular curves and straight lines or a polygon that you create.

Drawing Lines and Arrows

The most basic drawing objects you create on your worksheets are lines and arrows. Excel includes several tools for this purpose. The Line tool creates line segments. The Drawing toolbar's Line Style and Dash Style tools determine the type of line used in any drawing object—solid, dashed, or a combination of solid and dashed lines. The Arrow tool lets you create arrows that emphasize key features of your worksheet.

> **TIP**   If the Drawing toolbar is not visible, choose View ➤ Toolbars ➤ Drawing.

Draw a Straight Line

1. Click the **Line** button ◻ on the Drawing toolbar.

2. Drag the pointer to draw a line on your worksheet.

3. Release the mouse button when the line is the length you want. The endpoints of the line are where you started and finished dragging.

Edit a Line

1. Click the line that you want to edit.

2. Click the **Line Style** button ▤ on the Drawing toolbar, and then select a line thickness.

3. Click the **Dash Style** button ▦ on the Drawing toolbar, and then select a dash style.

4. Click the **Line Color** button drop-down arrow ✐▾ on the Drawing toolbar, and then select a line color.

5. Drag the sizing handle at either end to a new location to change the size or angle of the line.

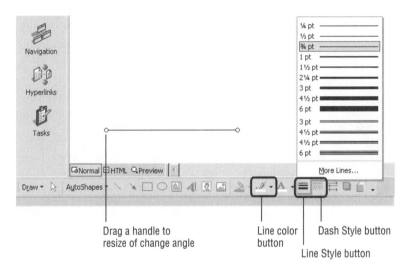

Drag a handle to resize of change angle

Line color button

Dash Style button

Line Style button

TIP You can use keys on the keyboard to adjust lines as you draw them. To constrain the angle of the line to 15-degree increments, hold down the Shift key on the keyboard as you drag the pointer. To draw the line from the center out, instead of from one endpoint to another, hold down the Ctrl key on the keyboard as you drag the pointer.

Draw a Curved Line

1. Click the **AutoShapes** button on the Drawing toolbar, and then point to **Lines**.

2. Click the **Curved**, **FreeForm**, or **Scribble** symbol.

3. To draw a curve, click a point on the screen, move the pointer. To draw a Freeform, click a point, move the pointer, and then click to draw a straight line or drag to draw freely. To draw a scribble, drag the pointer.

4. Click the **Line Color** button on the Borders toolbar to select a line color.

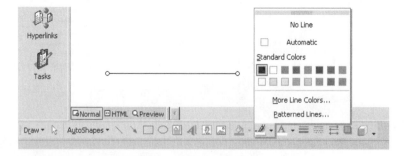

Drawing AutoShapes

You can choose from many different AutoShapes on the Drawing toolbar, ranging from hearts to lightening bolts. The two most common AutoShapes, the oval and the rectangle, are available directly on the Drawing toolbar. The rest of the AutoShapes are organized into categories that you can view and select from the AutoShapes menu. Once you have placed an AutoShape on a worksheet, you can resize it using its sizing handles (small white squares that appear along the edge of an object). Many AutoShapes have an *adjustment handle*, a small yellow diamond located near a sizing handle, which you can drag to alter the shape of the AutoShape.

> **TIP** To draw a perfect circle or square, click the Oval button or the Rectangle button on the Drawing toolbar, and then hold down the Shift key on the keyboard as you drag the shape.

Draw an Oval or Rectangle

1. Click the **Oval** button or the **Rectangle** button on the Drawing toolbar.

2. Drag the pointer across the worksheet where you want to place the oval or rectangle.

3. Release the mouse button when the object is the shape you want. The shape assumes the line color and fill color defined by the presentation's color scheme.

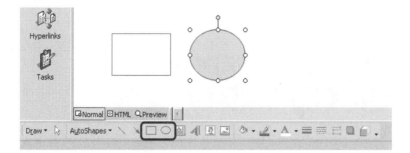

Draw an AutoShape

1. Click the **AutoShapes** button AutoShapes ▾ on the Drawing toolbar, and then point to the AutoShape category you want to use.

2. Click the symbol you want.

3. Drag the pointer across the worksheet until the drawing object is the shape and size that you want.

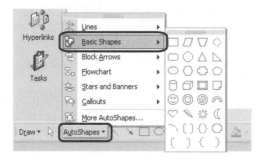

> **NOTE** You can replace one AutoShape with another and retain the size, color, and orientation of the original shape. Click the AutoShape you want to replace, click the Draw button on the Drawing toolbar, point to Change AutoShape, and then select the new AutoShape.

Adjust and Resize an AutoShape

1. Click the AutoShape you want to adjust.

2. Click one of the adjustment handles (white circle), and then drag the handle to alter or resize the form of the AutoShape.

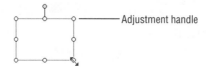
— Adjustment handle

Inserting AutoShapes from the Clip Gallery

Clips
Artwork you can insert from the Clip Gallery.

In addition to drawing AutoShapes, you can insert AutoShapes, such as computers and furniture, from the Clip Gallery. These AutoShapes are called **clips**. The Clip Gallery displays a miniature of each clip. You can drag the clip onto your worksheet or click the clip to select other options, such as previewing the clip or searching for similar clips.

> **TIP** To view the full More AutoShapes dialog box, click the Change To Full Window button on the toolbar.

Insert an AutoShape from the Clip Gallery

1. Click the **AutoShapes** button AutoShapes ▾ on the Drawing toolbar, and then click **More AutoShapes**. The Insert Clip Art task pane opens.

2. In the **Search text** box, type AutoShapes, and then click the **Search** button.

3. If necessary, scroll to display more AutoShapes.

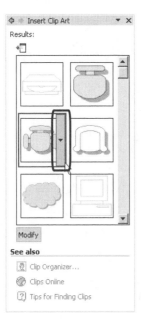

4. Drag the shape you want onto your worksheet.

5. When you're done, click the **Close** button ❌ to close the task pane.

> **TIP**
> You can import pictures into the Clip Organizer. Choose Insert ➤ Pictures. In the Insert Clip Art task pane, click Clip Organizer. In the Microsoft Clip Organizer window, choose File ➤ Add Clips To Organizer ➤ On My Own, select the file you want to insert, and then click the Add button. Click the Close button in the Microsoft Clip Organizer window.

Moving and Resizing an Object

After you create a drawing object, you might need to change its size or move it to a different worksheet location. Although you can move and resize objects using the mouse, if you want more precise control over the object's size and position, select the object and choose Format ➤ AutoShape to specify the exact location and size of the drawing object.

> **NOTE** You can use the Nudge command to move drawing objects in tiny increments, up, down, left, or right. You can nudge a selected object by holding down the Ctrl key on the keyboard, and then pressing an arrow key.

Move an Object

1. Position the pointer over the object you want to move. The pointer changes to a four-headed arrow.

2. Drag the object to a new location on the worksheet. Make sure you aren't dragging a sizing handle or adjustment handle. If you are working with a freeform object and are in Edit Points mode, drag the interior of the object, not the border, or you will end up resizing or reshaping the object, not moving it.

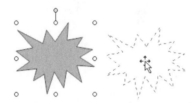

Resize a Drawing Object with the Mouse

1. Click the object you want to resize.

2. Drag one of the sizing handles.

    ◇   To resize the object in the vertical or horizontal direction, drag a sizing handle on the side of the selection box.

    ◇   To resize the object in both the vertical and horizontal directions, drag a sizing handle on the corner of the selection box.

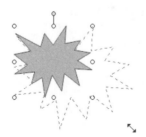

TIP To retain the proportions of the object you're resizing, hold down the Shift key on the key-board as you drag the object to its new size.

Rotating and Flipping an Object

You can change the orientation of a drawing object by rotating or flipping it. For example, if you want to create a mirror image of your object, you can flip it. To turn an object on its side, you can rotate it 90 degrees. Rotating and flipping tools work with drawing and text objects. You won't usually be able to rotate or flip objects such as charts and pictures.

Rotate an Object to Any Angle

1. Click the object you want to rotate.

2. Click the **Draw** menu on the Drawing toolbar.

3. Point to **Rotate Or Flip**, and then click **Free Rotate**.

4. Drag a rotation handle to rotate the object.

5. Click anywhere on the worksheet to set the rotation.

TIP To quickly rotate an object, select it, and then drag the green circle handle, which is connected to an object with an additional line.

Rotate or Flip a Drawing Using Preset Increments

1. Click the object you want to rotate.

2. Click the **Draw** menu on the Drawing toolbar.

3. Point to **Rotate Or Flip**, and then click one of the Rotate or Flip commands.

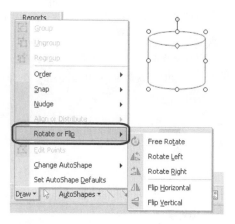

TIP   To constrain the rotation to 15-degree increments, hold down the Shift key on the keyboard when you rotate the object.

Choosing Object Colors

When you create a closed drawing object, you can select a fill color and a line color. When you create a drawing object, Excel uses the default color scheme to determine the line style and fill color. You can change the line and fill color settings using the same color tools you use to change a text color. You can also add fill effects, such as gradients, patterns, and clip art pictures.

TIP   To set a drawing object's default color and line style, right-click the object, and then click Set AutoShape Defaults on the shortcut menu.

Change a Drawing Object's Fill Color

1. Click the object whose fill color you want to change.

2. Click the **Fill Color** button drop-down arrow 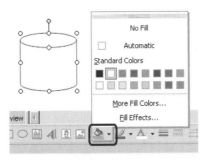 on the Drawing toolbar.

3. Select the fill color or fill effect you want.

Create a Line Pattern

1. Click the object that you want to modify.

2. Choose **Format ➤ AutoShape**, or right-click the object, and then click **Format AutoShape**. The Format AutoShape dialog box opens.

3. Click the **Line Color** drop-down arrow ▼, and then select **Patterned Lines**. The Patterned Lines dialog box opens.

4. Click the **Foreground** drop-down arrow ▼, and then select the color you want as a foreground.

5. Click the **Background** drop-down arrow ▼, and then select the color you want as a background.

6. Click the pattern you want from the Pattern grid.

7. Click the **OK** button to close the Patterned Lines dialog box.

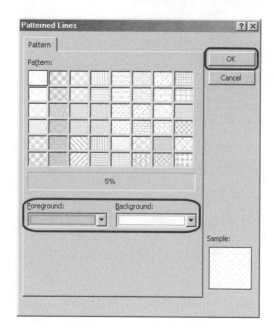

8. Click the **OK** button to close the Format AutoShape dialog box.

Adding Object Shadows

You can give objects on your worksheet the illusion of depth by adding shadows. Excel provides several preset shadowing options, or you can create your own by specifying the location and color of the shadow.

Use a Preset Shadow

1. Click the object to which you want to add a preset shadow.

2. Click the **Shadow Style** button [icon] on the Drawing toolbar.

3. Click a preset shadow styles or click Shadow Settings for more options.

Creating a 3-D Object

You can use the 3-D tools to add a three-dimensional appearance to objects. You can transform most AutoShapes into 3-D objects. You can create a 3-D effect using one of the 20 preset 3-D styles, or you can use the 3-D tools to customize your own 3-D style. You can control several elements using the customization tools, including the angle at which the 3-D object is tilted and rotated, the depth of the object, and the direction of light falling on the object.

Apply a Preset 3-D Style

1. Click the object to which you want to apply a preset 3-D style.

2. Click the **3-D Style** button on the Drawing toolbar.

3. Click a preset 3-D styles or click 3-D Settings for more options.

Aligning and Distributing Objects

When you work with two or more similar objects, you need to ensure that they look good on the worksheet. Objects often look best when you align them in relation to each other. For example, you can align three objects so that the tops of all three objects line up along an invisible line. Other times, you may want to distribute objects evenly across an area. Excel includes commands to distribute your items horizontally and vertically, and you can specify whether you want to distribute objects in their currently occupied space or across the entire worksheet.

TIP If the Drawing toolbar is not open, choose View ➢ Toolbars ➢ Drawing.

Align Objects

1. Hold down the Shift key on the keyboard while you click the objects that you want to align.

2. Click the **Draw** menu on the Drawing toolbar, and then point to **Align Or Distribute**.

3. Click the alignment option you want.

◇ **Align Left** lines up the left edges of the selected objects.

◇ **Align Center** lines up the centers of the selected objects.

◇ **Align Right** lines up the right edges of the selected objects.

◇ **Align Top** lines up the top edges of the selected objects.

◇ **Align Middle** lines up horizontally the middles of the selected objects.

◇ **Align Bottom** lines up the bottom edges of the selected objects.

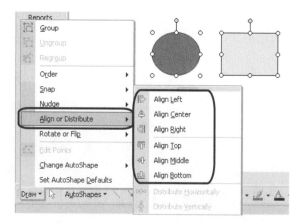

NOTE When you drag an object, you can instruct Excel to snap the object you're dragging to another object or to an invisible grid on the worksheet. Click the Draw menu on the Drawing toolbar, point to Snap, and then click To Grid or To Shape.

Arranging and Grouping Objects

You can insert multiple objects in a worksheet and create interesting effects by adjusting how they interact with each other. If you overlap the objects, Excel will place the most recently created object on top of the others. You can also change the order of the objects in the stack. You can group several objects so that you can move, resize, or copy them as a single unit.

Change the Order of Objects

1. Click the drawing object you want to place.

2. Click the **Draw** menu on the Drawing toolbar, and then point to **Order**.

3. Click the stacking option you want.

◆ Click **Bring To Front** or **Send To Back** to move the drawing to the top or bottom of the stack.

◆ Click **Bring Forward** or **Bring Backward** to move a drawing up or back one location in the stack.

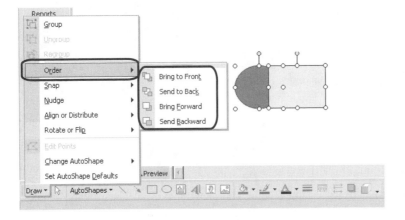

Group Objects Together

1. Hold down the Shift key on the keyboard while you click the objects that you want to group.

2. Click the **Draw** menu on the Drawing toolbar.

3. Click **Group**.

> **TIP** Align objects before you group them in order to ensure the best visual effect.

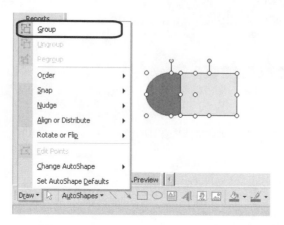

Ungroup a Drawing

1. Select the object you want to ungroup.

2. Click the **Draw** menu on the Drawing toolbar.

3. Click **Ungroup**.

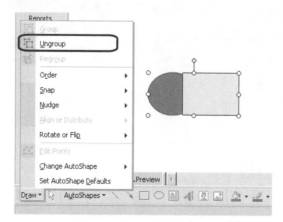

9 Adding Functionality to Web Pages

So far, you examined many of the key features available for Web masters in FrontPage. Now it's time to deal with key Web site components that usually require extensive HTML programming expertise. Using FrontPage, you can easily add these components to give your Web site a professional look with minimal effort and no programming expertise.

You will be working with what FrontPage calls Components—Shared Borders, Page Banners, Navigation Bars, and Hit Counters—as well as features such as annotated comments and online surveys. FrontPage pre-fabricates these features. Using FrontPage, you can place these components directly on your Web page through the Insert menu. In this chapter, you will learn about components, and also be introduced to some administrative tools like comments, that will help you manage the development of your web.

Annotating Web Pages with Comments

Developing a Web site can get involved, with a lot of tasks to be done. While developing the content on your Web page or site, you might want to attach comments in certain areas to help keep track of everything. This becomes more important when more than one person is working on the Web page or site.

Add a Comment to a Web Page

1. In Page view, position the insertion point where you want to add a comment.

2. Choose **Insert** ➢ **Comment**. The Comment dialog box opens.

3. In the **Comment** box, enter the comment.

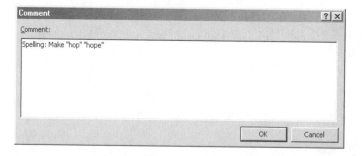

4. Click the **OK** button. The comment is inserted on the page in a different color than the text so that it stands out when you are editing your pages.

Comments are not visible in the Web browser of a Web site visitor, but they *do* appear on screen if the visitor decides to view your page source, so practice discretion when writing comments.

TIP   To edit a comment, display the page with the comment you want to change in Page view, double-click the comment, edit the comment, and then click the OK button.

Working with Page Banners

Page banners are blocks of text, such as headlines, column and section headers, and the Web site name. Page banners maintain the styles and graphics of a theme if you are using one. If you are not using themes, you enter the text and then format it yourself by selecting the font, style, and size. A good way to add banners to more than one page is to position the banner inside a shared border or frame.

Insert a Page Banner

1. In Page view, position the insertion point where you want to place the page banner.

2. Choose **Insert** ➢ **Page Banner**. The Page Banner Properties dialog box opens.

3. Click the **Picture** option or the **Text** option button, and then enter the text for the banner.

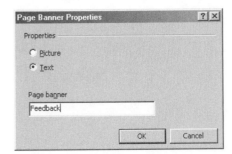

4. Click the **OK** button. If you selected the Text option, the text you entered for the banner appears as a placeholder on the page. If you selected the Picture option, the stylized, graphically-enriched version of your banner appears on the page.

Graphic banner

Edit and Format a Page Banner

1. In Page view, right-click the banner you want to edit, and then click Font on the shortcut menu. The Font dialog box opens, displaying the Font tab.

2. Select the font settings you want, if necessary.

3. Click the **Character Spacing** tab.

4. To change character spacing, click the **Spacing** drop-down arrow ▾, select a spacing option (either **Normal**, **Expanded**, or **Condensed**), and then enter the amount of spacing you want in the **By** box.

5. To change character position, click the **Position** drop-down arrow ▾, and then select a positioning option (either **Baseline**, **Sub**, **Super**, **Top**, **Text-Top**, **Middle**, **Bottom**, or **Text-Bottom**).

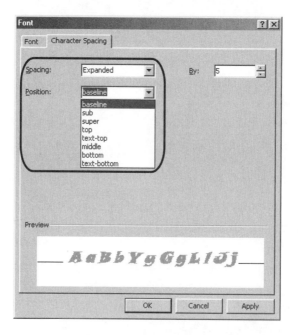

6. When the text looks right, click the **Apply** button, and then click the **OK** button. The Banner is now revised.

Inserting Scheduled Images

A Scheduled Image is a graphic element that may or may not be on screen at any given time. These images are scheduled to appear at fixed intervals or at a single preset time (such as when you have prepared a new page and you want the Web site to update to that page at a specific time).

Insert a Scheduled Image

1. In Page view, position the insertion point where you want to display the graphic.

2. Choose **Insert ➢ Web Component.** The Insert Web Component dialog box opens.

3. In the left pane, click **Included Content.** The currently scheduled content is displayed in the window on the right pane in the dialog box.

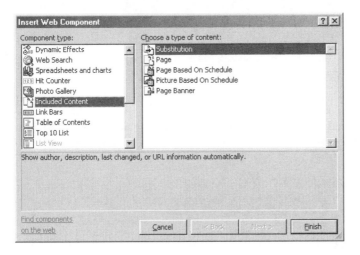

4. In the right pane, click **Page Based On Schedule** to import a Web page or click **Picture Based On Schedule** to import a picture, and then click the **Finish** button. For purposes of illustration, click **Picture Based On A Schedule**. The Scheduled Picture Properties dialog box opens.

NOTE All the Included Content options open the same dialog box, except for Page Banner, which opens the Page Banner Properties dialog box.

5. In the **During The Scheduled Time** box, type the Relative URL (the Net address of a page relative to the address of the current page), or click the **Browse** button, locate and select a photo, and then click the **OK** button.

6. Enter the **Starting** and **Ending** times in the appropriate boxes.

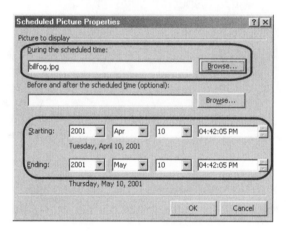

7. Click the **OK** button. The picture you selected now appears in the pre-selected position. The picture will now appear and re-appear based on the schedule you selected.

 The clock that is used to time the appearances of graphics is based on the Web server's clock.

Inserting Timestamps

A Timestamp is a FrontPage component that displays the date, time, or both, when the page was either created or last revised. Timestamps are easy ways for visitors to tell if the Web site's been updated since their last visit.

Insert a Timestamp

1. In Page view, position the insertion point where you want to place the timestamp.

2. Choose **Insert** ➢ **Date and Time**. The Date and Time dialog box opens.

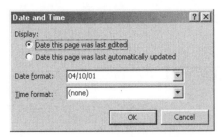

3. Click one of the display option buttons.

4. Click the **Date Format** drop-down arrow ▼, and then select a format, and click the **Time Format** drop-down arrow ▼, and select a format, if necessary.

5. Click the **OK** button.

Inserting a Table of Contents

The next two components you'll be learning about are important to the organization of a web. The Table of Contents, for example, not only lets visitors know what's on your Web site, but tells users where to find it.

You can base your Table of Contents (TOC) on either the categories assigned to your pages or the navigational structure of your Web site. A TOC based on the navigational structure might also include pages containing hyperlinks that are not included in the navigational structure, so a visitor can click any feature listed in the TOC and be transported directly to that location. The TOC need not occupy an entire page, though it can be assigned its own page. This is usually determined by how much content your Web site contains. The TOC can be edited and formatted. FrontPage even offers the option of automatically resetting the TOC whenever an editorial change is made.

A site map, meanwhile, provides a navigation-style, page-by-page guide of your entire site. A site map is especially helpful on large Web sites with numerous parent and child pages covering everything from original content and visitor feedback to staff biographies and linked Web sites.

In fact, small, personal Web sites might comprise no more than a series of hyperlinks to the web's various pages, and this type of site map can be generated through the Table of Contents component.

Create a Table of Contents

1. In Page view, position the insertion point where you want to produce the table of contents.

2. Choose **Insert** ≻ **Web Component**. The Insert Web Component dialog box opens.

3. In the left pane, click **Table Of Contents**. The list of Table of Contents options appears in the right pane.

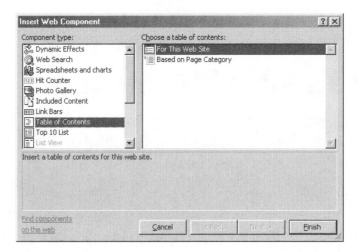

4. In the right pane, click **For This Web Site**, and then click the **Finish** button. The Table of Contents Properties dialog box opens.

5. In the **Page URL For Starting Point Of Table** box, enter the relative URL of the page that serves as the starting point for the TOC. You can also click the **Browse** button to locate the page you want.

TIP The point where you place the insertion point will represent the left border of the TOC.

---

6. In the **Heading Font Size** box, select the size of the styled text you want to use in your header.

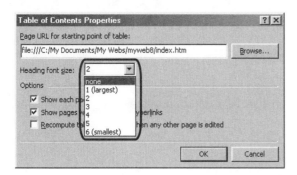

If you are creating a table of contents on the same page as the starting point (your home page, or Index.htm) you will want to avoid creating a link that connects a page to itself. Therefore, click None in the Heading Font Size box.

7. In the Options area, select the options you want.

◆ Select the **Show Each Page Only Once** check box if your Web site contains pages that are linked to multiple hyperlinks, but you want the TOC to only list each page once.

◆ Select the **Show Pages With No Incoming Hyperlinks** check box to include pages that are not pointed to by any of the hyperlinks in your web.

◆ Select the **Recompute Table Of Contents When Any Other Is Edited** check box to automatically edit and reconfigure your TOC when any page in your web is edited. This can be an extensive and lengthy procedure. It is usually easier to manually reset the TOC by saving and opening the page containing the TOC.

8. Click the **OK** button. The Table of Contents is inserted into the page.

Create a TOC from Categories

1. Click the **Folders** button on the **Views** bar, right-click a page you want to assign to a category, and then click **Properties**. The Page Properties dialog box opens.

2. Click the **Workgroup** tab.

3. In the **Available Categories** box, click the category you want to assign to this page.

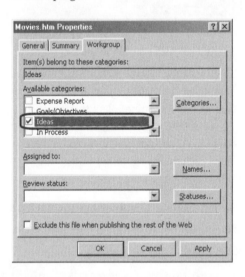

NOTE   If you want to add or remove a category, click the Categories button on the Workgroup tab. The Master Category List dialog box opens. You can now enter a new category, and then click the Add button, or select a category, and then click the Remove button. Click the OK button to return to the Page Properties dialog box.

---

4. Click the **OK** button. The category is assigned.

5. Repeat the first four steps for each page that you want to assign to a category.

6. In Page view, position the insertion point where you want your TOC located.

7. Choose **Insert ➤ Web Component**. The Insert Web Component dialog box opens.

8. In the left pane, click **Table Of Contents**, and then click **Based On Page Category** in the right pane.

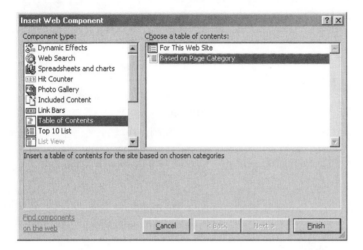

9. Click the **Finish** button. The Categories Properties dialog box opens.

10. Select the categories whose pages you want to include in your table of contents. These selected categories will appear in the **Selected Categories** box.

11. The **Sort Files By** box offers two options:

    ◇ **Document Title** sorts the list alphabetically

    ◇ **Date Last Modified** sorts the list, in ascending order, by date

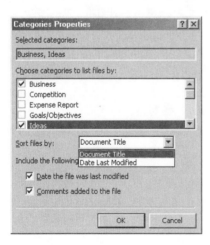

12. To display the **Date The File Was Last Modified** or **Comments Added To The File**, check the appropriate option.

13. Click the **OK** button. Your table of contents slot appears in Page view.

NOTE

To test your Table of Contents, click Preview In Browser.

Create a Site Map

Site maps can be based on categories. But for purposes of organization, you must first designate each of the categories. Begin by creating a category on your site map.

NOTE

If the categories you want to use on your site map have already been added to the list of available categories or you're using categories from the Available Categories list, you can skip the following section.

1. Click any button on the Views bar, except Tasks.

2. Right-click any page, and then click **Page Properties**. The Page Properties dialog box opens.

3. Click the **Workgroup** tab.

4. Click the **Categories** button to create a category. The Master Category List dialog box opens.

5. In the **New Category** box, enter the name of the category you want to use on your site map.

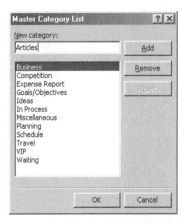

6. Click the **Add** button to add the category to the master category list, and then click the **OK** button. The category has now been added to your site map.

7. In the Folder list, right-click the page you want to categorize, and then click **Properties** on the shortcut menu.

8. Click the **Workgroup** tab.

9. In the **Available Categories** list, select the check box of the category in which you want to group the page.

10. Create a new page or open an existing page to which to add the site map.

11. In the Normal pane, position the insertion point where you want to add the first category list.

12. Type the name of the category as a heading for the list of files in that category. Continue entering categories to complete the site map.

Inserting Navigation Bars

The larger the Web site, the more important it is that visitors be able to navigate easily through your Web site. One of the most effective tools in that area is the Navigation Bar, a FrontPage component that can be positioned in the shared border area of your Web pages. A Navigation Bar is actually a collection of hyperlinks used to guide visitors through a Web site. The hyperlinks usually lead to primary pages, such as a contact page or the site's home page. Link bars can be placed on every page of your Web site, so visitors can always navigate easily without getting lost in a maze of pages. These bars can also have buttons and text hyperlinks.

You can create buttons, much as you can create hit counters, or you can set up your web's navigation system and have FrontPage automatically generate the link bars for you.

NOTE Link bars can only be generated when you are working within a Web site, not on separate pages.

There are three types of link bars.

◇ **Custom Link Bar**—Import any Web pages from your Web site or external sites. This type of link bar can be set up on a custom basis, and you're free to add or remove pages at any point.

◇ **Link Bar With Back And Next Links**—Uses your navigation system to track the last page that a visitor has read as well as the next page in the Web site.

◇ **Link Bar Based On Your Site's Navigation Structure**—Uses the Navigation view structure to determine which hyperlinks to include on its bar and what to call them.

Add a Link Bar

1. In Page view, position the insertion point where you want to place the link bar.

2. Choose **Insert ➤ Navigation**. The Insert Web Component dialog box opens.

3. In the right pane, click **Bar With Custom Links**.

4. Click the **Next** button. The next Insert Web Component dialog box opens with a selection of link bar styles.

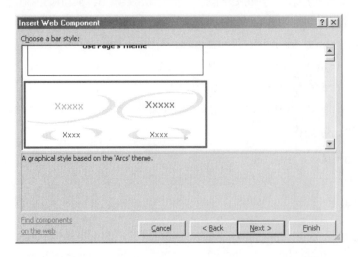

5. Select the link bar style you want to use, and then click the **Next** button. The next Insert Web Component dialog box opens with a selection of orientations for the link bar.

6. Select the orientation for the link bar.

7. Click the **Finish** button. The Link Bar Properties dialog box opens.

8. To create a new link bar, click the **Create New** button, enter a name for your new link bar, and then click the **OK** button. The Link Bar Properties dialog box opens.

9. Click the **Add Link** button. The Add To Link Bar dialog box opens.

10. Browse to locate the page you want to add, and then double-click it to close the Add To Link Bar dialog box and add the link.

11. Click the **OK** button. The Link Bar Properties dialog box closes. The page appears with + Add Link as a placeholder.

Change Link Bar Properties

1. In Page view, right-click the link bar, and then click **Link Bar Properties**. The Link Bar Properties dialog box opens, displaying the General tab.

2. Select the options you want.

◆ To add a link, click the **Add Link** button, select the new link, and then click the **OK** button.

◆ To remove a link, select the link you want to delete, and then click the **Remove Link** button.

◆ To change a link, click the **Modify Link** button, make your changes, and then click the **OK** button.

3. Click the **Style** tab, and change the settings you want for the link bar.

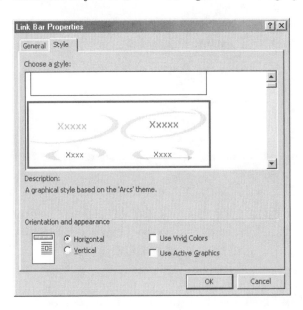

4. Click the **OK** button.

Creating Discussion Groups

As Web master, it's your assignment to provide a forum for those visitors who want to discuss subjects related to your web. You will want to add hyperlinks that take readers to related materials on certain subjects; provide a search engine so visitors can locate the subjects they have interest in; and some form of message board so that visitors can post their thoughts.

Now, set up the possibility of creating a discussion group based on your Web site (Remember that some of this material might not be supported by all browsers.)

Create a Discussion Group

1. Choose **File** ➢ **New** ➢ **Page Or Web**. The New Page Or Web task pane opens.

2. Under New from Template in the New Page Or Web task pane, click **Web Site Templates**. The Web Site Templates dialog box opens.

3. Click **Discussion Web Wizard**. To add this template to your web, select the **Add To Current Web** check box to select it.

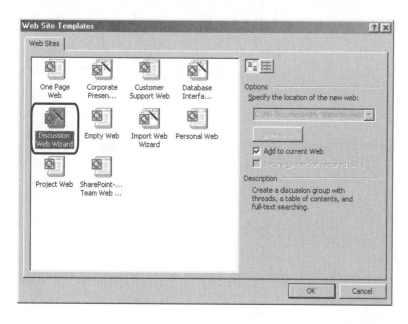

4. Click the **OK** button. The Discussion Web wizard opens.

5. Read the opening comments, and then click the **Next** button.

6. Select the check boxes with the main features you want in your discussion, and then click the **Next** button.

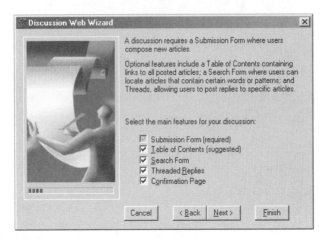

Adding a Table of Contents will make it easy for users of your discussion forum to find the content they are interested in reading. A Search form will let them quickly search existing posts for a topic they want to view, or comment on. Threaded replies keep original posts and all replies to them (even replies to the replies) in a single grouping. Confirmation page, when selected, provides a page for users to review their posts before they actually get published on the Web site.

7. Enter a name that will appear on the Web site for the discussion forum, name the folder that will contain the discussion, and then click the **Next** button.

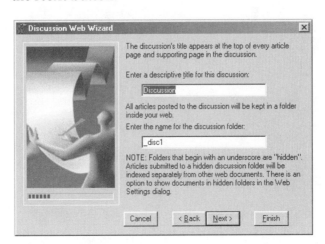

8. Choose the input fields that the user must complete to post to the forum. For most non-commercial Web sites, the **Subject, Comments** option works best. Click the **Next** button.

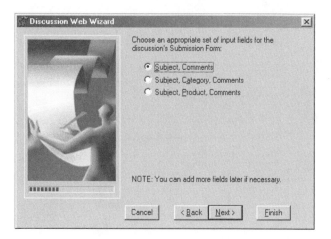

9. Determine whether this will be an open forum to all users, or a closed forum where users must input a password to participate, and then click the **Next** button.

10. Determine whether posts should be displayed from most current to oldest, or oldest to most current from top to bottom on the page, and then click the **Next** button.

11. Select whether you want the Table of Contents for the discussion forum to be the home page of the web (this would only be appropriate if the discussion was the central focus of the Web site), and then click the **Next** button.

12. Select the information you want the Search Form to report for matching document.

13. If the option appears and you do not want to use a theme, simply click the **Next** button to skip this step. To apply a theme to the discussion Web, click the **Choose Web Theme** button. The Choose Theme dialog box opens. Select themes and properties that you want to use, and then click the **OK** button. The Choose Theme dialog box closes and the Discussion Web wizard continues.

14. Determine whether or not to apply frames to the discussion Web, and then click the **Next** button.

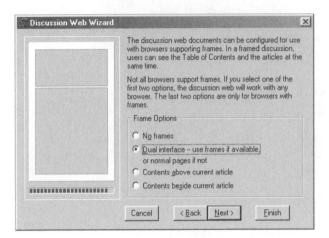

15. You have completed all the necessary steps for the wizard, click the **Finish** button to view your finished discussion Web.

Inserting Online Surveys

Surveys are useful in many ways to the proprietor of a successful Web site. You get to find out how people feel about your various components and, more important, you find out about your visitors. Good survey responses tell you the demographics of your visitors, and as many other questions as you want to ask. Assuming that your Web site is using a server that runs Microsoft's Share-Point Team Services, begin by creating a survey.

To insert an online survey:

1. Choose **File ➢ New ➢ Survey**.

2. Double-click **New Survey Wizard**. The New Survey Wizard dialog box opens.

3. Click the **Next** button as you complete each step in the dialog box.

4. In the **Name** box, enter a name for the survey, and then describe it briefly in the **Description** box. Click the **Next** button, then click the **Add** button.

5. In the **Question Text** box, enter a sample question.

6. In the **Information Type** section, select the type of answer you want produced from your reader responses. Type refers to data type, as in Boolean, Currency, Integer, or String type. Boolean type, for example, is based on what is called if-then logic. Using this type you can set conditions for the survey, such as "If you required information on stock conditions, what Web site would you go to?"

7. Click the **Finish** button. You can then repeat the process of asking questions an infinite number of times.

8. Set the permission settings and options for the survey. Determine who will have access to which survey entries, etc.

When you are finished, a survey folder, that contains various forms for working with the survey, is added to the folder list on your web.

10 Gathering User Input Using Forms

In this chapter, you're going to create Web page forms. Forms that appear on Web pages are similar to paper forms. Web page forms share the same purpose (gathering information about your visitors) and use many of the same devices (check boxes, information fields, etc.) as paper forms. The most popular types of forms include:

- ◇ Request
- ◇ Registration
- ◇ Feedback
- ◇ Contact information
- ◇ Survey
- ◇ Guest book
- ◇ Order (shipping and billing information)
- ◇ Log On (prompts visitors to enter name and password)
- ◇ Search (enables visitors to search your site)

Understanding Form Fields

One of the keys to creating a form is the creation of fields. There are many different types of fields, including text boxes, text areas, option buttons, drop-down menus, and push buttons.

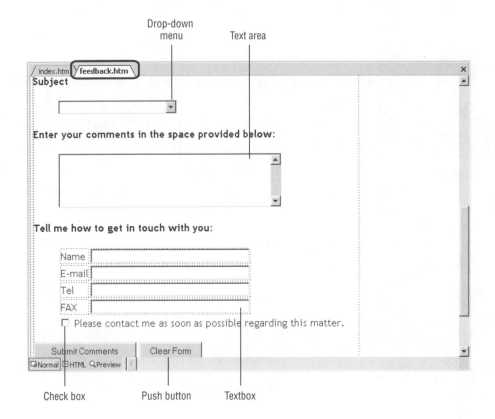

In addition to these fields, there are also Advanced Buttons, which you can customize through font and color selection, and Group Boxes, which you use to segregate clusters of related controls into one group. Password fields are basically one-line text boxes used to add passwords to your site so that you can restrict access (to charge for membership, for example). When a site visitor enters their password, it appears on screen as a collection of asterisks to secure confidentiality.

After you've decided what types of fields to add to the form, you define what you want them to do and how you want them to look. You can even set properties for each field, such as the length of a text field, or the available options on a drop-down menu. After you create a form, you have to determine how to collect and display the visitor data.

Validating Forms

To make sure that the visitor fills out the forms correctly, you will have to set data entry rules, a process also known as Validation. You can further guide the user by setting the format in which the data is accepted. If you're asking for a telephone number, for example, set up your text box so that it only accepts numbers and hyphens. You can also pre-set the number of character spaces so the visitor doesn't inadvertently leave out or add a number.

After you've collected the information, you need to access it. FrontPage offers form handlers, server programs that are executed when a form is submitted to your site. Using these form handlers you can produce a database of visitor information and even offer users access to special features. You can have the results saved (or e-mailed) as either a text or HTML file.

You can also add a confirmation page (the form the visitor has just filled out is displayed and the visitor is given the opportunity to either edit or confirm it); create keyboard shortcuts (displayed as an underlined letter in the field label); or allow visitors to navigate the form using the Tab key.

NOTE   Your server will require either FrontPage Server Extensions or SharePoint Team Services for the FrontPage forms to function on your Web site. Your web administrator or ISP can let you know whether this software is included on your server.

NOTE   Microsoft Windows 2000 security and Microsoft Internet Information Services (IIS) do not allow registration through a web browser.

Creating Forms

FrontPage offers numerous types of forms so that you can collect information from visitors to your site. You can start from scratch and create the form by adding information fields to a blank form, or you can use one of the wizard templates. When you first create a form, FrontPage inserts a rectangular box with a perforated line-dash perimeter. Inside this box, you can add everything from check boxes and text fields to drop-down boxes and submit buttons.

Create a Form Using a Wizard

1. In Page view, choose **File** ➢ **New** ➢ **Page Or Web**. The New Page Or Web task pane opens.

2. In the New Page Or Web task pane, click **Page Templates**. The Page Templates dialog box opens.

3. Click the **General** tab, and then click the **Form Page Wizard** icon.

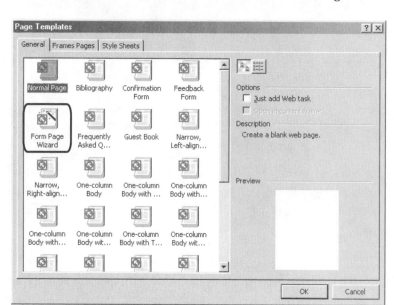

4. Click the **OK** button. The Form Page Wizard opens.

5. Read the instructions, and then click the **Next** button. This takes you to a dialog box that allows you to add questions to the form and maintains a list of them. Click the **Add** button for a list of potential new questions. The next Form Page Wizard dialog box opens so that you can select the type of input you want to collect.

6. Select the type of input you want, and then click the **Next** button. The next Form Page Wizard dialog box opens so that you can select input options.

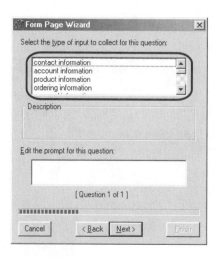

7. Select the items you want to collect from users, and then click the **Next** button.

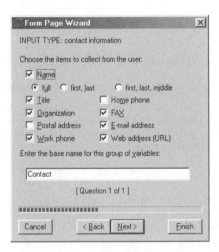

8. Repeat the cycle, adding more questions, and then click the **Finish** button.

Create a Form

1. Click **Page** button on the Views bar.

2. Choose **Insert ➢ Form**. The Form submenu opens.

NOTE If an item on the Form submenu is grayed out, the command is not available. You need a Web server equipped with FrontPage Server Extensions or SharePoint Team Services to active the commands.

3. Click **Form**. A rectangular box with a perforated line-dash perimeter appears, accompanied by two push buttons, labeled Submit and Reset.

TIP To remove a form field, including the push buttons, click the field to select it in Page view, and then press the Delete key.

4. To add space before or after the push buttons, so you can insert other form fields, click to place the insertion point before or after the buttons, and then press the Enter key as necessary.

NOTE When inserting a form field before you've created the form, FrontPage automatically creates a form area and places it within the form. While editing the page, the form border appears as a perforated line.

Inserting Text Boxes

You can insert two types of text boxes in a form, Textbox and Text area. Textboxes ask for information and provide a field where a visitor can type an answer. Textboxes are used for collecting relatively small quantities of information, such as the visitor's online name. Text areas are small text windows best-suited for brief text entries. This window scrolls vertically and horizontally to maximize its available space. They are ideal for use as guest books.

Insert a Text Box or Text Area

1. In Page view, position the insertion point in the form where you want to place the textbox or text area.

2. Choose **Insert** ➤ **Form** ➤ **Textbox** or **Text Area**. A text box or text area appears in the form.

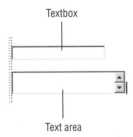

Textbox

Text area

You can click to place the insertion point before or after the text box.

3. Type the label next to the box.

Labeled textbox

Change Text Properties

1. In Page view, double-click the text box or text area. A Text Properties dialog box opens.

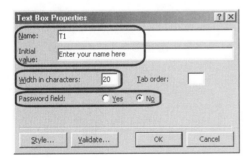

2. In the **Name** box, enter a name that will identify the textbox.

NOTE The textbox name will be transparent on the form but will be visible to site visitors on the default confirmation page if you use a form handler (a server program that runs whenever a visitor submits a form) rather than a custom script.

3. In the **Initial Value** box, enter the text to be displayed in the text box when a site visitor first opens the form. As you type, the characters will be counted in the **Width In Characters** box.

4. For text boxes, click the **Yes** option button to create a password to your Web site so that you can restrict access (to charge for membership, for example). When a Web site visitor enters their password, it appears on screen as a collection of asterisks to secure confidentiality.

5. Click the **OK** button.

Inserting Check Boxes

Check boxes are provided to allow users multiple choices from a list or series of options. Check boxes are just what they sound like—a statement which you either confirm, by checking the box, or decline by leaving the box blank.

Insert a Check Box

1. In Page view, position the insertion point in the form where you want to place the check box.

2. Choose **Insert** ➤ **Form** ➤ **Check box**. A check box appears in the form.

Checkbox

3. Type the check box label next to the box.

☐ Do you want to register on this site?

Checkbox with label

Change Check Box Properties

1. In Page view, double-click the check box you want to change. The Check Box Properties dialog box opens.

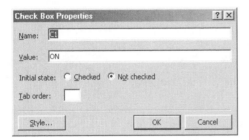

2. In the **Name** box, enter a name that identifies the check box in the form results. The name is not displayed on the form.

3. In the **Value** box, enter a value to associate with the check box. This value is returned with the form results and is displayed on the default confirmation page.

4. In the Initial State area, click the **Checked** option or the **Not Checked** option button to set up the default state when a visitor opens the form.

5. Click the **OK** button.

Adding Option Buttons

Option buttons (also known as Radio Buttons) are used when asking a visitor a question with more than one possible answer.

Add an Option Button

1. In Page view, position the insertion point in the form where you want to place the option button.

2. Choose **Insert ➢ Form ➢ Option Button**. The option button appears in the form.

Option Button

225

3. Type the text that you want to appear with the option button.

Option Button and Label

| TIP | To change option button properties, double-click the option button, change options in a similar way as a check box, and then click the OK button. |

Activating a Label

After you type a label next to a check box or option button, you can specify whether Web site visitors select the check box or option button by clicking the box or button, or its label. If you want your visitors to click the label, you need to active the label.

Activate a Label

1. In Page view, select both the text and the check box or option button to which you want to activate the label.

Checkbox and label selected

2. Choose **Insert** ➢ **Form** ➢ **Label**. The text label appears surrounded by a perforated border, which indicates the label is active.

Text in perforated border

Inserting Drop-Down Menus

Drop-down boxes are used when the user must select one item from a list. By clicking the down arrow to the right of the box, a menu opens revealing a list of selections. You can only select one item from the list.

Insert a Drop-Down Menu

1. In Page view, position the insertion point in the form where you want to place the drop-down menu.

2. Choose **Insert** ➢ **Form** ➢ **Drop-Down Box**. The drop-down box appears on the form.

3. Type the text that you want to appear with the drop-down box.

Drop-down box and label

4. Double-click the drop-down box. The Drop-Down Box Properties dialog box opens.

5. In the **Name** box, enter a name, following the same rules you applied to the previous components.

6. Click the **Add** button to add selections to display on your drop-down menu. The Add Choice dialog box opens.

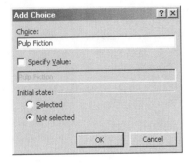

7. In the **Choice** box, type the name of the choice.

8. In the Initial State area, click the **Selected** option or the **Not Selected** option button to set up the default state when a visitor opens the form.

9. Click the **OK** button. The Add Choice dialog box closes. The choice appears in the Drop-Down Box Properties dialog box.

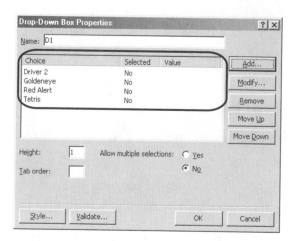

10. Repeat the process until you have specified all of the choices that you want to appear on the form, and then click the **OK** button. The drop-down menu appears in the form.

Inserting Push Buttons

Push buttons are functional components that are used when the visitor needs to do something. When you insert a form field, two buttons appear, Submit and Reset. The Submit button is a command that a visitor has to click to submit the form when completed, while the Reset button is a command that a visitor has to click to reset the form and start over. You can create a push button to perform an action.

> **NOTE** Remember that you'll need either SharePoint Team Services of FrontPage Server Extensions to really test your buttons' functions.

Insert a Push Button

1. In Page view, position the insertion point in the form where you want to place the push button.

2. Choose **Insert** ➤ **Form** ➤ **Push Button**. A push button appears in the form.

Push Button

3. Double-click the push button. The Push Button Properties dialog box opens.

4. In the **Name** box, enter a name that identifies the push button in the form results. The name is not displayed on the form.

5. In the **Value/Label** box, type the label that appears on the button.

6. In the **Button Type** area, click the button type you want (**Normal** is the standard button, **Submit** is a button that submits the completed form, or **Reset** is a button that clears the form so the visitor can start over).

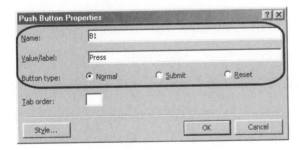

TIP   If you are familiar with HTML, you can return to Page view, and then click the HTML tag to write a specific script in HTML to influence your button's action.

---

7. Click the **OK** button.

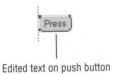

Edited text on push button

Inserting a File Upload

The file upload form field is used so that visitors can send a file to your web. The visitors begin by clicking the Browse button, selecting the file, then clicking either Submit or (if there was an error) Reset. To insert a file upload form field, position the insertion point in the form where you want to place the push button, and then choose Insert ➢ Form ➢ File Upload.

Inserting Pictures

You can insert a picture in a form, which you can use as a button. If you want, you can use a picture button, like a push button, to perform an operation. You insert a picture in a form in a similar way you insert a picture in a Web page.

Insert a Picture

1. In Page view, position the insertion point in the form where you want to place the picture.

2. Choose **Insert ➢ Form ➢ Picture**. The Picture dialog box opens.

3. Locate and select the picture you want to use, and then click the **Insert** button. The picture appears as a button in the form.

Blue Planet

TIP To change the name that identifies the picture in the form results, right-click the picture button, click Form Field Properties, enter a name in the Name box, and then click the OK button.

Formatting Form Fields

After you create a form field, such as a text box, text area, option button, drop-down menu, or push button, you can format the text associated with the field in the same way you format any other text using formatting dialog boxes.

Format a Form Field

1. In Page view, double-click the form field you want to format. A Properties dialog box opens.

2. Click the **Modify Style** button. The Modify Style dialog box opens.

3. Click the **Format** button. A shortcut menu opens.

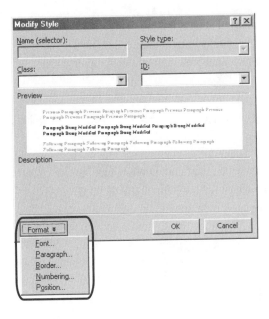

4. Click a formatting command (**Font**, **Paragraph**, **Border**, **Numbering**, and **Position**). A formatting dialog box opens.

5. Make the formatting selections you want.

6. Click the **OK** button twice.

Setting Rules for Entering Data

For some form fields—textbox, text area, option button, or drop-down box—you can set rules that visitors to your Web site are required to follow to provide consistent results for gathering data.

Set a Rule for Entering Data

1. In Page view, double-click the form field (textbox, text area, option button, or drop-down box) to which you want to set rules. A Properties dialog box opens.

2. Click the **Validate** button. The Validate dialog box opens.

3. Select the options you want to set rules for entering data.

   ♦ For a drop-down box or option button, click the **Data Required** check box to select it.

   ♦ For textbox or text area, click the **Data Type** drop-down arrow ▼, select the type of data you require in the text box, and then select other related options.

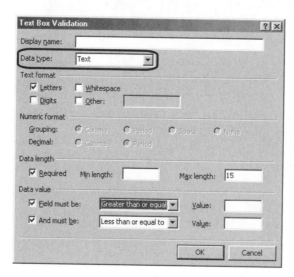

232

4. Click the **OK** button twice.

Connecting a Form to a Database

When you have a lot of data about your site visitors, you'll want to save that information so that you can use the content. You can save the information in a form to a database by creating a database connection. A database connection is a connection that specifies the name, location, and type of database you want to access. FrontPage comes with a wizard that creates one form for the visitor submit information and another form you to track the results.

NOTE To view the data once you set up the connection, your web site must be hosted or published on a Web server configured with Active Server Pages (ASP), Active Data Objects (ADO), FrontPage 2000 Server Extensions or later or SharePoint Team Services, and Internet Information Server (IIS) version 4.0 (or later).

Connect a Form to a Database

1. Choose **File** ➢ **New** ➢ **Page Or Web**. The New Page Or Web task pane opens.

2. In the New Page Or Web task pane, click **Web Site Templates**. The Web Site Template dialog box opens.

3. Click the **Database Interface Wizard** icon, click the **Add To Current Web** check box to select it, and then click the **OK** button. The Database Interface Wizard opens.

4. Click the **Create A New Access Database Within Your Web** option button to create a new database, or click the **Use An Existing Database Connection** option button and select a database from the drop-down menu. Click the **Next** button.

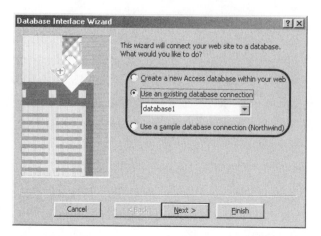

5. Type a name for the database or select the table or view you want to use, and then click the **Next** button.

6. Edit the list of columns and submission fields for the database using the **Add**, **Modify** and **Delete** buttons, and then click the **Next** button.

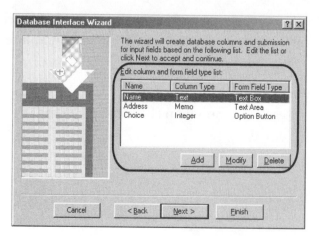

7. Click the **Next** button again to display a series of additional optional database pages that the wizard can create.

8. Select the additional pages that you want to create, and then click the **Finish** button. The standard Database Interface page opens.

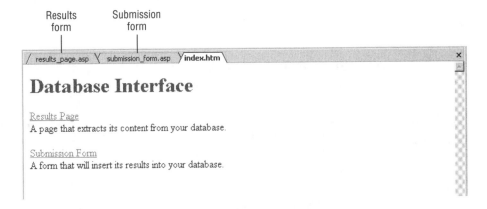

> **NOTE** Instead of creating an entire set of forms, you can also set up a database connect to an area in a form. To set up a database connection, choose Insert ➤ Database ➤ Results. The Database Results Wizard dialog box opens. Click the Use A New Database Connection option button or the Use An Existing Connection option button, and then follow the wizards instructions to create an new database or use an existing database, specify the record source that contains the information you want, fields that will display the database results, and formatting options for the records.

Saving Form Results

Once you create a form and collect information from visitors on the Web, you can save the form results to a database or file, or send the form results in an e-mail message. You can save the results to an ODBC-compliant database or a text or HTML file. When a site visitor fills out a form and submits it, FrontPage enters the data directly into a database or file, or sends an e-mail message. By default, form results are saved to a text file.

Save Form Results to a Database

1. In Page view, right-click the form you want to save the results from, and then click **Form Properties** on the shortcut menu. The Form Properties dialog box opens.

2. Click the **Send To Database** option button, and then click the **Options** button. The Options For Saving Results To Database dialog box opens.

> **NOTE** To create a new database, click the Create Database button. A message box opens, displaying the name and Web location of the database. Click the OK button twice.

3. Click the **Database Connection To Use** drop-down arrow ▾, and then select an existing database connection.

4. Click the **Table To Hold The Form Results** drop-down arrow ▾, and then select the table where you want to place the form results data from.

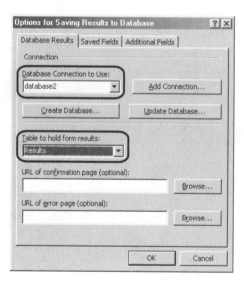

5. Click the **Saved Fields** tab. The fields in the form are listed. For each field, you must specify the database column in which you want to save the data.

6. In the **Form Fields To Save** box, click a form field, and then click the **Modify** button. The Modify Field dialog box opens.

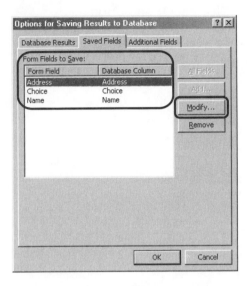

7. Click the **Save To Database Column** drop-down arrow 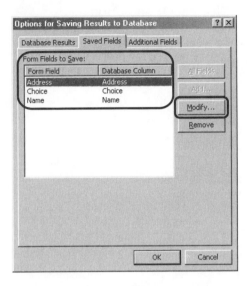, and then select the column in which you want to save form field data, and then click the **OK** button.

> **TIP**
> To save additional information to your database (timestamp, user name, etc.), click the Additional Fields tab in the Options For Saving Results To Database dialog box, and then click the type of additional information you want to save in the Additional Fields To Save list.

8. Repeat steps 6 and 7 for each form field, and then click the **OK** button to close the Options For Saving Results To Database dialog box.

9. Click the **OK** button to close the Form Properties dialog box.

Save Form Results to a File

1. In Page view, right-click the form, and then click **Form Properties** on the shortcut menu. The Form Properties dialog box opens.

2. Click the **Send To** option button. A default name and results location appears.

3. Click the **Options** button. The Saving Results dialog box opens.

4. Click the **File Results** tab.

5. In the **File Name** box, enter the location and name of a new file, or click **Browse** button, locate and select the file to which you want to save the results, and then click the **Open** button.

6. Click the **File Format** drop-down arrow 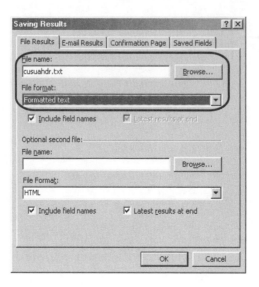, and then select a file format (such as **HTML** or **Formatted Text**).

7. Click the **OK** button to close the Saving Results dialog box.

8. Click the **OK** button to close the Form Properties dialog box.

Send Form Results as E-Mail

1. In Page view, right-click the form, and then click **Form Properties** on the shortcut menu. The Form Properties dialog box opens.

2. Click the **Send To** option button.

3. In the **E-Mail Address** box, type the e-mail address to which you are sending the form results.

4. Click the **File Name** field if you do *not* want the results saved to a file as well as being sent via e-mail.

5. Click **Options**. The Saving Results dialog box opens.

6. Click the **E-Mail Results** tab.

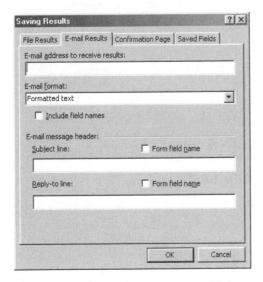

7. Perform one or more of the following steps:

   ◇ In the **E-mail Format** box, select the text format you want from the drop-down menu.

   ◇ In the **Subject Line** box, type the text that you want in the subject line of the e-mail (the default subject line in the e-mail is Form Results).

   ◇ If you want the subject line of the e-mail to contain the results of one field from the form, click the **Form Field Name** check box to select it, and then type the name of the field in the Subject Line box.

   ◇ In the **Reply-To Line** box, a specific e-mail address can appear as the sender of the e-mail (the From or Reply To line in the e-mail). Enter the address.

   ◇ If the form contains a field that collects the site visitor's e-mail address, that address can be used as the sender's address. Click the **Form Field Name** check box to select it, and then type the name of the form field in the Reply-To Line box.

8. Click the **OK** button to close the Saving Results dialog box.

9. Click the **OK** button to close the Form Properties dialog box.

Creating a Custom Form Handler

You can also set up a form to save results using a custom form handler. A form handler is a program on a server that is executed when a site visitor submits a form. You can use your custom script (ISAPI, NSAPI, CGI, or ASP Script) as a form handler.

Create a Custom Form Handler

1. Click the **Folders** button on the Views bar.

2. Right-click the folder that contains the script, and then click **Properties** on the shortcut menu. A dialog box opens containing the name of your page followed by the word Properties.

3. Click the **Allow Scripts To Be Run** check box to select it.

4. If you want other users to be able to view files in your directory, click the **Allow Files To Be Browsed** check box to select it.

5. Click the **OK** button.

6. Click the **Page** button on the Views bar.

7. Right-click the form, and then click **Form Properties** on the shortcut menu. The Form Properties dialog box opens.

8. Click the **Send To Other** option button, click the drop-down arrow ▾, and then click **Custom ISAPI, NSAPI, CGI, or ASP Script** formats.

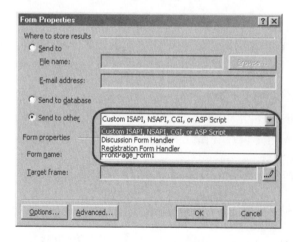

9. Click **Options**. The Options For Custom Form Handler dialog box opens.

10. Click the **Method** drop-down arrow ⏷, and then select one of the following formats for submitting data to the form handler.

   ◆ **Get**—Encodes the form's name-value pair and assigns the data to a server variable named Query_String.

   ◆ **Post**—Passes the name-value pair to the form handler as input.

   ◆ **Default**—Leaves the Encoding Type text box empty.

11. Click the **OK** button to close the Options For Custom Form Handler dialog box.

12. Click the **OK** button to close the Form Properties dialog box.

Creating and Attaching a Confirmation Page

Use Form Confirmation Pages so that your site visitors can confirm that the information they've entered on a form is correct and, if changes need to be made, the visitors can reset the form and begin again.

Create and Attach a Confirmation Page

1. Choose **File** ➢ **New** ➢ **Page Or Web**. The New Page Or Web task pane opens.

2. In the New Page Or Web task pane, click **Blank Page**. A blank page opens.

3. Enter the text you want displayed after a visitor has submitted a form anywhere on the page, and then select the text.

4. Choose **Insert** ➢ **Web Component**. The Insert Web Component dialog box opens.

5. In the left pane, click **Advanced Controls**.

6. In the right pane, double-click **Confirmation Field**. The Confirmation Field Properties dialog box opens.

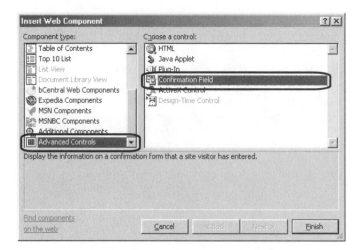

7. In the **Name Of Form Field To Confirm** box, enter the form field from which to display your information. This name must match the name you assigned the form field when you selected its properties.

8. Click the **OK** button. The name of the field is displayed in brackets on the form. When the confirmation form is displayed to a site visitor, the field displays the visitor's entry.

9. Repeat these steps for each field you want to display. Fields can also be hidden if you don't want them displayed.

11 Publishing and Managing a Web Site

• •

Now that you know how to plan, build, and run a Web site, the only areas that remain are publishing and managing the Web site. Publishing a Web site is the process of copying all of the files that make up a web to a predetermined destination, while managing a Web site is the process of administering the day-to-day maintenance, which includes viewing reports and creating, assigning, and performing tasks.

Publishing a Web Site

Publishing a Web site refers to the process of copying all of the files that make up a web to a predetermined destination. In FrontPage, you typically publish your site for one of two reasons. The first reason is to launch the site on either a company intranet (a network limited to members of a specific group, usually a business) or on the World Wide Web. The second reason is to back up the site on either your computer or a network drive. Using the FrontPage Publish Web command you can publish all your web files, only those that have been edited, or individual files. You can publish your web files to a folder on your local or network drive, or on a Web server. When you publish a site, FrontPage maintains all the hyperlinks, as well as the original web's theme.

Using FrontPage Server Extensions or SharePoint Team Services

The reasons in favor of publishing to a server equipped with Microsoft's FrontPage Server Extensions 2002 or its SharePoint Team Services are profound and obvious.

1. You have the advantages associated with running your FrontPage created site on a server with functionality designed to best complement and empower it. Also, servers without those extensions will not generate the site as you created it, because not all of the features will work. The lack of form handlers, category-based site maps, and hit counter components deprives you of several key tools from the FrontPage virtual workshop.

2. With access to the Microsoft programs, FrontPage maintains your files and hyperlinks, updating any changes whenever you publish the site.

3. FrontPage can publish your Web site using HTTP. Or, you can use FrontPage to publish your web to an FTP server.

4. There are several ways to publish your web to a variety of locations. A disk-based site hosted on a local computer, for example, can be converted to a server-based site hosted by a Web server by following the instructions for publishing through HTTP.

5. You can update your link bars on the server to match any changes you made to the Web site on your local computer.

Publish a Web Site

1. Choose **File ➢ Open Web**, locate and select the Web site you want to publish, and then click the **Open** button. The Web site opens.

2. Choose **File** ➢ **Publish**. The Publish Destination dialog box opens.

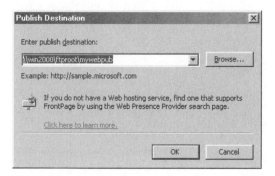

3. In the **Enter Publish Destination** box, type the location and name of a folder on a local or network drive, or on a Web server that has Front-Page Server Extensions.

4. Click the **OK** button. If the folder location doesn't exist, a message dialog box opens, asking to create one. Click the **Yes** button. The Web Publish dialog box opens.

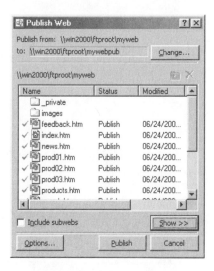

5. Click the **Publish** button.

6. If the Web site contains dynamic FrontPage components, the Publishing FrontPage Components dialog box opens. Click the **Continue** button.

7. When the publishing process is done, a message dialog box opens, displaying links to open the Web site or a log file. Click a link or the **Done** button.

Entering the Publish Destination

When you publish your site to a folder on your local file system, you enter a location using the syntax *C:\\sitefolder*, where *C* is the drive letter. When you publish your site to a folder on a network server, you enter a location using the Universal Naming Conventions (UNC). UNC is a file-naming convention that produces a machine-independent way to locate a file. The UNC name employs the syntax *server\share\path\foldername*. When you publish your site to a folder on a Web server on the World Wide Web, you enter a Uniform Resource Locator (URL). A URL consists of three parts: the prefix *http://*, which indicates a Web address; a network identification, such as *www* for World Wide Web; and a Web site name, or domain name, such as *microsoft.com*.

Publish a Web Page

1. In the Folders or Reports view, and then select the Web pages you want to publish.

2. Right-click the selected pages, and then click **Publish Selected Files**. The Publish Destination dialog box opens.

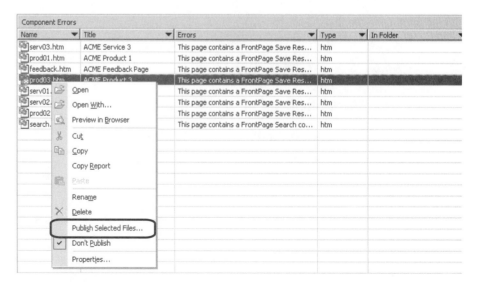

3. In the **Enter Publish Destination** box, type a folder location, if necessary.

4. Click the **OK** button. The Web Publish dialog box opens.

Updating a Web Site

Historically, a site that does not periodically update its material will not attract many repeat visitors. Housekeeping, therefore, is a crucial component of Web maintenance. You can opt to publish only those files that have been edited or altered in some way. FrontPage can compare the files in the working site on your local computer to the published files on the server, and determine if changes have been made on each file. If it detects a more recent version on your computer, that's what gets published.

You can also choose which files you don't want to publish. For example, if a page is incomplete, not directly part of your Web site, or simply out-of-date, you can mark the file as Don't Publish.

Update a Web Site

1. Choose **File ➤ Open Web**, locate and select the Web site you want to update, and then click the **Open** button. The Web site opens.

2. In Page view, modify the Web pages you want to update.

3. Choose **File ➤ Publish**. The Publish Destination dialog box opens. A check mark appears next to files that need to be updated.

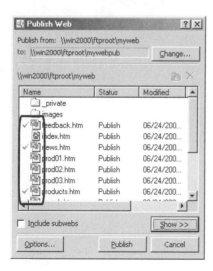

4. Click the **Options** button. The Options dialog box opens, displaying the Publish tab.

5. Click the **Changed Pages Only** option button, if necessary.

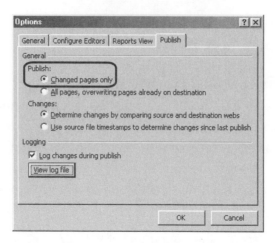

6. Click the **OK** button to close the Options dialog box.

7. To mark a file as don't publish, right-click the Web page you don't want to publish, and then click **Don't Publish**. A small stop sign icon is added to the Web page icon.

8. Click the **Publish** button, and then click the **Done** button when the Web pages are updated.

Deleting a Web Site

Before the discussion of deleting sites, a word of warning—always back up your files before deleting a Web site or sub-web. After you delete a web or sub-web, it is gone, and no number of Undo commands can restore it. Also, if you produced the Web site in question by converting a folder on a local computer into a site, that folder and all of its contents will be permanently deleted from that computer. To delete a web or sub-web, or a sub-web, open the web in Folder view, right-click the web or sub-web, and then click Delete. You cannot delete a sub-web unless you have administrative status from the parent Web site.

Checking Web Settings

If you need to find out the name of your Web server, version of your FrontPage Server Extensions or server, you can use the Web Settings command on the File menu. You can also rename your Web site.

Check Web Settings

1. Choose **Tools** ➢ **Web Settings**. The Web Settings dialog box opens, displaying the General tab, which indicates the Web name, FrontPage Server Extensions version, and server version.

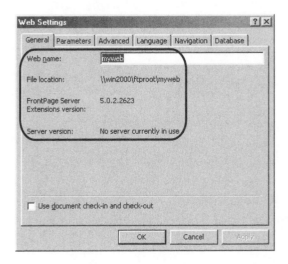

2. To rename the web, enter a new name in the **Web Name** box.

3. Click any of the other tabs (**Parameter**, **Advanced**, **Language**, **Navigation**, and **Database**) on the Web Settings dialog box, and then select the options you want.

4. Click the **OK** button.

Viewing Reports for a Web Site

Site reports can offer extensive information and records regarding your site's performance and its visitors. With FrontPage, you can generate reports on a wide variety of on-site activities.

- ✧ Monitor Web Site Usage—Reports that keep a record of items such as most popular pages and types of browsers used to visit your site.

- ✧ View A Web Site Summary—Provides general data regarding your site's content, from the number of files to a list of hyperlinks on your site.

- ◆ View Maintenance Problems—Produces reports on maintenance problems, such as large pages (big files download slowly) or pages containing broken hyperlinks.

- ◆ Manage Workflow—Reports that help you manage your workflow (to make sure pages aren't too long or are inconsistent in size) by showing the status of your Web pages. Files in your site can be categorized, assigned to different authors, or checked in and out using source control.

Web site reports come in several different types.

- ◆ The Site Summary report displays an overview of your site's vital statistics, from number of files to number of hyperlinks.

- ◆ File Status reports the age of all files, who is assigned to them, when they were last edited, and when they first appeared on your site. It reports on: All Files, Recently Added Files, Recently Changed Files, and Older Files.

- ◆ Maintenance Problems reports on display-related problems on your site, such as component errors, files that are taking too long to download, or broken hyperlinks. It reports on: Unlinked Files, Slow Pages, Broken Hyperlinks, and Component Errors.

- ◆ Workflow Status reports on file status and assignments in your site, including review status, the person the file is assigned to, and so on. It reports on: Review Status, Assigned To, Categories, Publish Status, and Checkout Status.

- ◆ Site Usage reports on visits to your site, including page hits, browsers used by site visitors, etc. It reports on: Usage Summary, Monthly Summary, Weekly Summary, Daily Summary, Monthly Page Hits, Weekly Page Hits, Daily Page Hits, Visiting Users, Operating Systems, Browsers, Referring Domains, Referring URLs, and Search Strings.

View Reports for a Web Site

1. Choose **View** ➤ **Reports**. A submenu appears, displaying a list of report types.

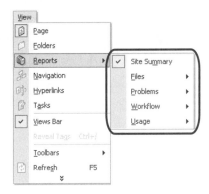

2. Point to a submenu to display a list of reports.

3. Click a report. The report opens.

4. To sort a report by a specific category, click the column header for the category, and then select a sort method.

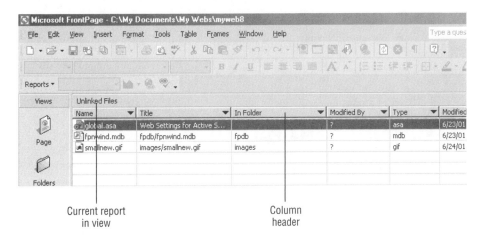

Current report
in view

Column
header

Change Reports View Options

1. Choose **Tools** ➤ **Options**. The Options dialog box opens.

2. Click the **Reports View** tab.

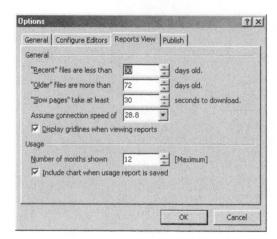

3. Enter the option changes you want.

 ♦ Recent files are less than a number of days old.

 ♦ Older files are more than a number of days old.

 ♦ Slow Pages take at least a number of seconds to download.

 ♦ Assume connection speed of 14.4, 28.8, 56.6, ISDN, T1, or T3.

 ♦ Number of months shown.

4. Click the **OK** button.

Creating and Assigning Tasks

Files can be assigned to an individual or to an entire workgroup. Within a workgroup environment, product managers assign files to different workgroups. Product managers can then monitor the progress of the workgroups through the Assigned To and Review Status reports. Within the Tasks view, the product managers can oversee the individual workgroup monitors as well as each assigned task.

When assigning a file, you can add a review status that explains the type of work done on the file. If a file requires a legal review, for example, create the review status legal review, indicate the file's status, and then assign it to the person responsible for accomplishing this task. When the legal review is complete, that person can classify the task as approved.

It's also possible to view your site's files on an assignment basis by using the Assigned To report, which displays your Web files by assignment. The Assigned To report displays these files in a column format and provides the following information:

- ◇ File name—File name
- ◇ Title—File title
- ◇ Assigned To—User name or workgroupto which the task is assigned
- ◇ Assigned Date—Date the file was assigned
- ◇ Assigned By—Who assigned the file
- ◇ Comments—Comments that describe work that needs to be done on a file, or any other information you feel is necessary
- ◇ Type—Type of file (.gif, .css, .htm, etc.)
- ◇ In Folder—Folder in the Web site where the file is stored

Files can be sorted in any column heading displayed in the Assigned To report. You can also filter the values displayed in any of the report columns. The filtering choices for that column can be obtained by clicking the column heading.

Tasks can be assigned to individuals or a workgroup and feature a description of the work comprising the task. When dealing with files (whether they're pictures, text, or sound bites), you associate a task and a file, and then assign it to yourself in the capacity of a co-worker.

In the Tasks view, you monitor the many tasks on your site. Tasks view uses a column format and provides status information about each task under these column headings:

- ◇ Status—Indicates whether the task is completed or in progress
- ◇ Task—Task name
- ◇ Assigned to—User name or workgroup to which the task is assigned
- ◇ Priority—High, medium, or low
- ◇ Associated with—Name of the file, if any, that the task is associated with
- ◇ Modified date—Last time the file was modified
- ◇ Description—Description of work that needs to be done, or any other information

Create and Assign a Task

1. Choose **File** ➤ **New** ➤ **Task**. The New Task dialog box opens.

2. In the **Task Name** box, enter a task name.

3. In the **Assigned To** box, enter (type or select) the name of the individual or workgroup to whom this task is being assigned.

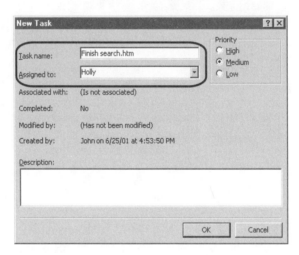

4. In the **Description** box, enter a description of the task. This field can be used to describe the work that needs to be completed on the task.

5. In the Priority area, click a priority option button (the default is Medium).

NOTE When you create a task in Page view while you're editing a page, that task is automatically associated with the page file. The name of the file associated with the task is displayed in the Associated With field.

6. Click the **OK** button.

NOTE To add a review status setting for a task, right-click the task you want to change in Tasks view, click Properties, click the Workgroup tab, click the Review Status drop-down arrow, and then select a status option.

Perform a Task

1. Click the **Tasks** button on the Views bar.

2. Right-click the task you want to perform, and then click **Start Task** on the shortcut menu. The task is performed. When you begin a task associated with a page, FrontPage automatically opens it in Page view.

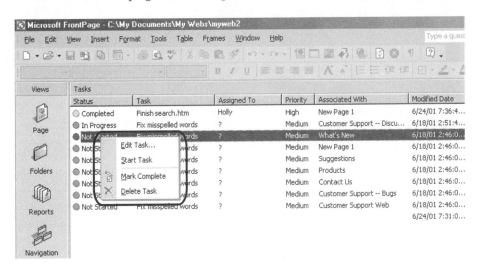

NOTE | When you begin a task associated with a different type of file, FrontPage opens the file in its associated editor (Word for .doc files, Notepad for .txt files, etc.). If the task is not associated with a file, the task is not performed.

NOTE | If you want to mark a task as complete, right-click the task in Tasks view, and then click Complete. If a task is designated as Completed, you can change its description but not its name.

View Task Assignments

1. Choose **View** ➢ **Reports** ➢ **Workflow** ➢ **Assign To**. Reports view appears, displaying task assignments.

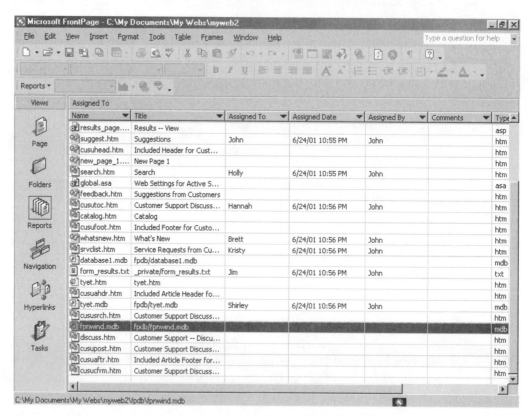

2. To sort choices in a report by the information in a column (Name, Title, Assign To, etc.), click the column heading.

Glossary

AutoShapes
Preset objects, such as arrows, common shapes, banners, circles, or callouts.

Bookmark
An internal link used to navigate between sections or topics within a lengthy web page.

Built-In Style
The formatting attributes available to you by default in the FrontPage Style list.

Cascading Style Sheet (CSS)
A document you use to maintain a consistent style throughout multiple Web pages and that gives you greater control over how your web is displayed in different browsers.

Cell
A single unit of a table, usually rectangle or square in shape.

Child page
Any page that links back to a Mother page or Parent page.

Clip art
Pre-drawn art that can be taken from a commercial source and inserted into your web.

Clips
Artwork you can insert from the Clip Gallery.

Column
A series of vertically-aligned cells within a table.

Cropping
The process of framing a portion of a photo and eliminating any unnecessary visual elements.

Delimited text
Text in which each data field is separated by a comma, paragraph, or other character.

Drag-and-drop
A technique for moving or copying data short distances.

Dynamic HTML (DHTML)
A Microsoft enhancement to HTML version 4.0 that enables you to create visual effects or improve the layout of a Web page.

Embedded CSS
When you create a new page, or modify the existing style of a page, FrontPage automatically creates an embedded CSS that contains all the code stored between the page's HTML tags

External CSS
Style sheets that can be linked to several Web pages so that you can apply a single style consistently throughout an entire web. If you make an alteration in your style, it only needs to be changed in the External CSS and the whole site automatically is updated. Most External CSS carry .css file extensions.

Freeform
A drawing with irregular curves and straight lines or a polygon that you create.

Frameset
A page that breaks up a browser window into several modular areas, or frames that are capable of independently displaying multiple Web pages.

Frames page
A form of HTML page containing no visible content that serves as a container that indicates which pages to display and where these pages should be displayed.

Hover button
A button that a site visitor can click to link to a page, sound, graphic, or other Web element.

HTML
The programming language used to create Web pages and Web sites. The abbreviation stands for hypertext markup language.

Hyperlinks
Links on your Web page that take you to another location in cyberspace.

Inline CSS
User-defined styles that are applied to a single-page element. This is the rarest type of CSS.

Inline Frame
A frames page with the contents embedded in an existing Web page.

Lines
Straight or curved lines (arcs) that connect two points.

Link bars
A collection of graphic or text buttons to hyperlinked pages both inside and outside your Web site.

Marquee
An animated banner commonly used in headers to draw attention to the title of the site.

Mother page
FrontPage's name for a site's original source page, the top page of the site, because all other pages in a web lead back to it.

Multitasking
The capability to open multiple pages or documents at the same time.

Office Assistant
An animated Help feature that displays helpful tips while you are working in FrontPage.

Office Clipboard
A temporary area that holds up to 24 pieces of copied information and is available from within any Office program.

Parent page

Any page within a web that has pages linked back to it.

Row

A series of horizontally-aligned cells within a table.

Shared borders

Areas of a page intended for content you want to appear on more than one of your Web pages.

Smart tag

A button that helps you control the results of certain actions, such as copy and paste or automatic text correction.

Style

A collection of formatting characteristics identified by a single name

Table

An orderly collection of information displayed within clearly-defined borders.

Template

A pre-formatted Web page or site.

Themes

Motifs that visually unify your site.

Thumbnail

A miniature depiction of a Web page graphic. It usually contains a hyperlink that leads to a larger version of the image.

URL

The code signifying a location or "address" in cyberspace.

User-Defined Style

A style that is at least partially designed by a user.

Views

The various layouts in which you can work on your web site.

Watermark

A graphic that appears in the background of a Web page, but does not scroll as the page scrolls.

Web page

A single document on the World Wide Web with its own unique URL (Uniform Resource Locator). Web sites generally contain several, linked Web pages.

Web site

A single page or collection of pages about a given topic or topics organized and published on the World Wide Web.

Wizard

A series of dialog boxes that leads you through a task.

WordArt

Text objects that you create with pre-defined effects.

Index

SPECIAL CHARACTERS

+ box (on Web pages), 20

NUMBERS

3D objects, 191

A

adjusting AutoShapes, 184
adjustment handles, 182, 184
Advance Buttons (on forms), 218
aligning
    cell contents, 131
    objects, 191, 192, 194
    text, 63–64
animation effects, text, 162, 176–177
annotating Web pages, 196
arranging objects, 193
arrows, drawing, 180
Ask a Question box, 26–27
asking questions, 25–27
Assigned To reports, 253
audiences, focusing on, 2
AutoFormat, formatting tables, 117
AutoShapes, 180, 258
    adjusting (resizing), 184
    drawing, 182–183
    inserting from the Clip Gallery, 184–185
    replacing, 184

B

background color
    for table cells, 131–132
    for Web pages, 156–159
background pictures, inserting, 160–161
background sound, adding, 168–169
banners. *See* marquees; page banners

beveled borders, for graphics, 94
blank pages, closing, 4
blinking text, 162
BMP format, 80
boldface, adding to text, 61, 162
bookmarks, 258
    creating/deleting, 38–39
    linking to, 104–105
    navigating to, 39
    renaming, 39
borders
    of cells, 131–132
    of frames, 134, 147
        displaying, 150–151
    for graphics, 93–94
    shared. *See* shared borders
brightness (of graphics), adjusting, 91–92
browsers, 102
    adding, 37
    frame compatibility, 135–136
    interactive lists editable in, 178
    previewing Web pages, 36–37
Built In Style, 66, 258
bulleted lists, creating/ending, 56–58
bullets, creating, 58
buttons
    hover buttons, 170–171
    navigation buttons, 13, 20
    picture buttons, 20, 230, 231
    push buttons, 218, 222, 228–229
    toolbar button ScreenTips, 25

C

cameras, inserting graphics from, 85, 166
capitalizing text, 162
captions (for pictures), 164
    adding, 167–168

captions (for tables)
  adding, 122–123
  deleting, 125
  moving/aligning, 123
Cascading Style Sheets (CSSs), 66, 258
categories (of Web pages)
  adding/removing, 206
  assigning pages to, 206
  creating, 208–209
  creating tables of contents based on,
    206–208
cell properties, changing, 111, 129–132
cells (in tables), 110, 258
  adding, 119–120
  aligning contents, 131
  background color, 131–132
  borders, 131–132
  coloring, 115–116
  deleting, 124
  entering text, 113–114
  filling with (copying) text, 125
  header cells, 131
  inserting graphics in, 126
  merging, 120, 122
  properties, changing, 111, 129–132
  resizing, 129
  selecting, 114
  span, 130
  splitting (dividing), 112, 120, 121
  wrapping text in, 131
characters
  selecting, 51
  tabs, 119
check boxes (on forms), 218
  inserting, 224
  labels, 226–227
  names and values, 225
Child pages, 21–22, 258
circles, drawing, 183
citation text, 163
Class Selectors, 66
clip art, 258
  inserting graphics from, 83–84

Clip Gallery, 184
  importing pictures into, 185
  inserting AutoShapes from, 184–185
Clipboard. See Office Clipboard
clips, 184, 258
  clip art, 83–84, 258
  linking to hover buttons, 170–171
  organizing, 84
  videos, 171–173
closing Web pages, 32
closing Web sites, 27–28
color palettes
  custom palettes, 158–159
  FrontPage palettes, 159
color templates, 116
coloring
  hyperlinks, 157, 163–164
  lines, 181, 188, 189
  tables/table elements, 115–116
  text, 157
colors
  accessing more, 157–158
  for backgrounds. See background
    color
  custom colors, 158–159
  fill colors, 188, 189
  line colors, 181, 188, 189
  special effects, 159
  transparent color in graphics,
    95–96
columns (in tables), 110, 258
  adding, 119–120
  coloring, 115–116
  deleting, 124
  resizing, 129
  selecting, 114
commands, ScreenTips, 25
comments (on Web pages), 196
company information, entering/editing, 10
components of Web sites, 195–216
confirmation pages
  for discussion group posts, 214
  for forms, 219, 241–242

connecting forms to databases, 233–235

constraining drawing, 181

constraining resizing, 187

content (of Web pages/sites), 2

    exporting, 47–48

    importing, 45–46

contrast (of graphics), adjusting, 91–92

converting graphic formats, 99–100

converting graphics to grayscale, 92

converting text to tables, 118–119

copying

    graphics, 88–89

    text, 52–56

        in tables, 125

    web content, 48

Corporate Presence Web Wizard, 5–11

cropping graphics, 86–87, 167, 258

CSSs (Cascading Style Sheets), 66, 258

curved lines, drawing, 182

custom colors/color palettes, defining, 158–159

custom form handlers, creating, 240–241

custom lists, creating, 178

D

data (in form fields)

    entry rules, 232–233

    validating, 219

database connections, 233

Database Interface Wizard, 233–235

databases

    connecting forms to, 233–235

    creating, 236

    saving field data to, 237

    saving form results to, 236–237

dates, inserting, 202–203

dates last modified, displaying, 9

definition text, 162

deleting (removing)

    bookmarks, 39

categories of Web pages, 206

Dynamic HTML effects, 177

files, 18

form fields, 222

frames, 148–149

hyperlinks, 41

tables/table elements, 124–125

Web sites/sub-webs, 248

delimited text, 258

    converting to tables, 118–119

DHTML effects toolbar, 176–177

discussion groups

    creating, 213–216

    user resources, 214

Discussion Web Wizard, 213–216

distributing objects, 191

dividing. *See* splitting

document tabs, navigating Web pages, 32–33

downloading graphics (pictures) from the Web, 82–83, 126

drag and drop, 258

    moving/copying text, 52, 54

drawing

    arrows, 180

    AutoShapes, 182–183

    circles, 183

    constraining, 181

    curved lines, 182

    lines, 180, 182

    ovals, 183

    rectangles, 183

    squares, 183

    tables, 111–113

drawing objects. *See* objects (drawing objects)

drop-down menus (on forms), 218

    inserting, 227–228

duplicating graphics, 127

Dynamic HTML effects, 258

    highlighting, 177

    inserting, 176–177

    removing, 177

E

e-mail addresses, linking to, 40, 41
e-mail messages
    saving form results as, 238–239
    from site visitors, storing, 9
editing
    frames pages, 149–153
    hyperlinks, 21
    inline frames, 143–144
    lines, 181
    target frames, 152–153
embedded CSSs, 66, 258
entering text, 50–51
    in tables, 113–114
envelope buttons, 20
EPS format, 80
erasing lines in tables, 112–113
exiting FrontPage, 27–28
exporting Web page content, 47–48
external CSSs, 66, 258
external Web pages, linking to, 40–41

F

Feedback Form, wizard options, 8–9
fields. *See* form fields
file formats
    hover buttons, 171
    See also graphics formats
File Status reports, 250
File Transfer Protocol (FTP), 42
file upload form fields, 230
files
    copying, 48
    displaying/opening/deleting, 18
    exporting, 47–48
    importing, 45–46
    inserting graphics from, 81–82, 165
    publishing, 243, 244–248
    reports, 250, 253
    saving form results to, 237–238
    tasks. *See* tasks (Web sites)

fill colors, 188, 189
fill effects, 188
filling cells with text, 125
finding and replacing text, 58–61
finding the right word, 73
flipping graphics, 96–97
flipping objects, 187, 188
Folder List, opening Web pages with, 31
folders
    copying, 48
    displaying, 18
    exporting, 47–48
    importing, 45–46
    opening Web pages in, 14–15, 30
    publish destinations, 245, 246
    for template-based sites, 18
Folders view, 18
Font dialog box, formatting text, 62–63
fonts
    changing/resizing, 61–63
    effects, 63, 161–163, 164
footers (Web pages), options, 9
form confirmation pages, 219
    creating, 241–242
form fields, 218
    data entry rules, 232–233
    data validation, 219
    file upload fields, 230
    formatting, 231–232
    inserting, 221–222
    labels, 226–227
    password fields, 218, 224
    removing, 222
form handlers, 219, 240
    creating custom form handlers,
      240–241
Form Page Wizard, 219–221
formatting
    form fields, 231–232
    page banners, 200
    tables, 116–117
    text, 61–63, 161–163

Web pages
    with cascading style sheets, 66
    with themes, 22–24
    See also special effects
forms (on Web pages), 217–242
    confirmation pages, 219, 241–242
    connecting to databases, 233–235
    creating, 219–222
    feedback forms, 8–9
    fields. *See* form fields
    inserting, 221–222
    saving results, 235–239
    search forms, 214
    types, 217
    validating, 219
frame properties, setting, 139–140, 150–152
frames, 133, 134
    adding Web pages in, 138
    borders, 134, 147
        displaying, 150–151
    browser support, checking, 135–136
    deleting, 148–149
    inline frames, 141–144
    margins, 152
    opening, 150
    for organization purposes, 138
    properties, 139–140, 150–152
    scroll bars, 152
    spacing, 150–151
    splitting, 147–148
    target frames, 134, 152–153
frames page templates, 134
    customizing, 139–141
frames pages, 133, 134, 259
    creating, 136–138
    editing, 149–153
    for organization purposes, 138
    saving as framesets, 145–146
framesets, 145, 259
    saving, 145–146
    saving Web pages within, 146

freeforms, 180, 259
FrontPage (Microsoft)
    exiting, 27–28
    overview, 1–28
    starting, 3–4
FrontPage Server Extensions
    publishing importance, 197, 219, 222, 233, 244
    version number, displaying, 249
FrontPage window, 3
FTP (File Transfer Protocol), 42

G

GIF format, 80
globe buttons, 20
graphics (pictures/images), 79–108
    background pictures, 160–161
    borders, 93–94
    brightness, 91–92
    captions, 164, 167–168
    contrast, 91–92
    converting to grayscale, 92
    copying, 88–89
    cropping, 86–87, 167, 258
    duplicating, 127
    editor, 100–101
    flipping, 96–97
    formats. *See* graphics formats
    hotspots, 105–108
    as hyperlinks, 94, 107
    hyperlinks in, 102–108
    importing into the Clip Gallery, 185
    inserting, 81–85, 165–166
        in tables, 125–127
    linking to hover buttons, 170–171
    low resolution graphics, 100, 102
    moving, 89
    photo galleries, 164–167
    picture buttons, 20, 230–231
    previewing, 81
    quality, 80, 100
    resizing, 86, 87–88, 167

graphics *(continued)*
  restoring to original state, 90
  rotating, 96–97, 167
  saving, 82
    formats, 80
  scheduled images, 201–202
  special effects, 89–97
  text, adding, 90–91
  transparent color in, 95–96
  uses, 80
  wash out effect, 93
  watermarks, 160, 260
  wrapping text around, 95
graphics editor, configuring, 100–101
graphics formats (properties), 80
  changing, 97–99
  converting, 99–100
grayscale, converting graphics to, 92
grid, snapping objects to, 192
Group Boxes (on forms), 218
grouping objects, 193–194

H

handles
  adjustment handles, 182, 184
  sizing handles, 182
handwritten text, inserting, 76–78
header cells, 131
headers (Web pages)
  marquees, 173
  options, 9
headings, creating, 66
Help, 25–27
Help menu, 25, 26
help topics, displaying, 26
hidden text, 162
hiding the Office Assistant, 27
hit counters
  creating, 197, 198
  inserting, 197–198
  testing, 198

home pages. *See* Mother pages
horizontal lines, adding/modifying, 68–69
hotspots, 105–108
  modifying, 108
  text hotspots, 105, 106–107
hover buttons, 170, 259
  inserting, 170–171
HTML (Hypertext Markup Language), 3, 259
  Dynamic HTML effects, 176–177
  and tabs, 119
  vs. XML, 73
HTML format, 34, 35
  displaying Web pages in, 34
HTML tags, 34
  displaying, 35
hyperlinks, 12, 259
  coloring, 157, 163–164
  displaying, 9, 19–20
  editing, 21
  in graphics, 102–108
  graphics as, 94, 107
  hotspots, 105–108
  including new pages in, 13
  on link bars, 209, 212
  removing, 41
  rollover effects, 164
  verifying, 19–21
Hyperlinks view, 18
Hypertext Markup Language. *See* HTML

I

ID Selectors, 66
Image maps, 105
Images folder, 18
importing pictures into the Clip Gallery, 185
importing Web site content, 45–46
indenting text, 65
inline CSSs, 66, 259
inline frame properties, changing, 143–144
Inline Frame Properties dialog box, 144

inline frames, 141–144, 259
    editing, 143–144
    inserting, 142–143
    option buttons, 142
Insert Hyperlink dialog box, options, 40, 41
inserting
    AutoShapes, from the Clip Gallery, 184–185
    background pictures, 160–161
    check boxes, 224
    dates, 202–203
    drop-down menus, 227–228
    Dynamic HTML effects, 176–177
    form fields, 221–222
    forms, 221–222
    graphics, 81–85, 165–166
        in tables, 125–127
    handwritten text, 76–78
    hit counters, 197–198
    hover buttons, 170–171
    inline frames, 142–143
    link bars (Navigation Bars), 210–211
    online surveys, 216
    option buttons, 225–226
    page banners, 199
    picture buttons, 230
    push buttons, 228–229
    scheduled images, 201–202
    tables, 110–111
    tables of contents, 204–208
    text boxes/areas, 222–223
    timestamps, 202–203
    video clips, 171–172
    WordArt text, 74–75
interactive help, 26–27
interactive lists, creating, 178
internal Web pages
    linking to, 102–104
    linking to the Web, 13
Internet protocols, 42
italics, adding to text, 61, 162

J
JPEG format, 80

K
keyboard shortcuts (on forms), 219

L
labels (for form fields), activating, 226–227
Language toolbar, 76
lines, 180, 259
    colors/coloring, 181, 188, 189
    drawing, 180, 182
    horizontal lines, 68–69
    patterns, 189–190
    styles, 180, 181
    in tables, erasing, 112–113
lines of text
    selecting, 51
    spacing, 63, 64
link bar properties, changing, 212
link bars (Navigation Bars), 134, 209–212, 259
    adding/removing/changing links, 212
    avoiding using, 138
    creating, 211
    inserting, 210–211
    types, 210
linking
    to bookmarks, 104–105
    to e-mail addresses, 40, 41
    to external Web pages, 40–41
    to internal Web pages, 102–104
    Web pages to the Web, 13
links. *See* hyperlinks
lists
    bulleted/numbered lists, 56–58
    interactive lists, 178
logos, displaying, 9
low resolution graphics, creating, 100, 102

M

Maintenance Problems reports, 250
managing Web sites, 243, 247–256
margins of frames, 152
Marquee Properties dialog box, 174–175
marquees, 259
    creating, 173–174
    customizing, 174–175
Menu bar, 3
merging cells, 120, 122
Mother pages (home pages), 21–22, 259
    wizard options, 6
movies. *See* video clips
moving
    graphics, 89
    objects, 185, 186–187
    text, 52–56
    text boxes, 107
    Web pages, 16–17
moving around tables, 114
multimedia inserts
    background pictures, 160–161
    background sound, 168–169
    photo galleries, 164–167
    sound effects, 170–171
    video clips, 171–173
multitasking, 30, 259
music, linking to hover buttons, 170–171

N

navigating
    to bookmarks, 39
    Web pages, 32–33
Navigation Bars. *See* link bars
navigation buttons (on Web pages)
    including new pages in, 13
Navigation view, 11, 21–22, 134
    including new pages on sites in, 13
moving Web pages, 16–17
    opening Web pages, 14–15, 30
network servers, publish destinations
    (locations), 245, 246

new features (Web pages), displaying, 7
New Page or Web task pane, 4
Normal view, displaying HTML tags, 35
nudging objects, 186
numbered lists, creating/ending, 56–58

O

objects (drawing objects), 179–194
    3D objects, 191
    aligning, 191, 192, 194
    categories, 180
    colors, 188–190
    distributing, 191
    flipping, 187, 188
    grouping, 193–194
    moving, 185, 186–187
    nudging, 186
    resizing, 185, 186–187
    rotating, 187–188
    shadows, 190
    snapping to other objects/the grid, 192
    stacking order, 193
    ungrouping, 194
Office Assistant, 25–27, 259
    options, 26
    showing/hiding, 27
Office Clipboard, 259
    moving/copying text, 55–56
online surveys (on Web sites), inserting, 216
opening
    files, 18
    frames, 150
    Web pages, 14–16
        multiple pages, 30–31
    Web sites, 14–16
option buttons (on forms)
    inserting, 225–226
    labels, 226–227
organizing clips, 84
ovals, drawing, 183
overlines, adding to text, 162

P

page banners, 199–200
    formatting, 200
    inserting, 199
    See also marquees
Page view
    displaying Web pages, 18
    opening Web pages, 15–16
pages, selecting text on, 52
paragraphs
    selecting text in, 51
    spacing/indenting, 63, 65
Parent pages, 21–22, 260
password fields (on forms), 218, 224
Paste Options button, 54
pasting items, 53–54, 56
patterns
    fill effects, 188
    line patterns, 189–190
photo galleries, creating, 164–167
photographs. *See* graphics (pictures)
picture buttons, 20
    inserting, 230
    names, 231
pictures. *See* graphics
planning Web sites, 2
PNG format, 80, 99
Preview tab, previewing Web pages, 36
Preview view, 36
previewing pictures, 81
previewing Web pages, 36–37, 42–43
Print Preview, 42–43
printing Web pages, 42, 43–44
Private folder, 18
products, displaying, 7–8
Products/Services page options, 7–8
publishing Web pages, 246–247
publishing Web sites, 243, 244–248
    destinations (locations), 245, 246
    file options, 244
    reasons for, 244

server requirements, 197, 219, 222, 233, 244
push buttons (on forms), 218, 222, 228
    inserting, 228–229
    scripting, 229

Q

questions, asking, 25–27

R

radio buttons, inserting, 225–226
RAS format, 80
rectangles, drawing, 183
renaming
    bookmarks, 39
    Web pages, 12
    Web sites, 249
replacing AutoShapes, 184
replacing text, 58–61
reports for Web sites, 249–252
    types, 249–250, 253
    view options, 251–252
    viewing, 251
Reports view, verifying hyperlinks, 20–21
Reset button (on forms), 222, 228
resizing
    AutoShapes, 184
    constraining, 187
    graphics, 86, 87–88, 167
    objects, 185, 186–187
    table elements, 129
    text boxes, 107
restoring task panes, 4
rollover effects (for hyperlinks), 164
rotating graphics, 96–97, 167
rotating objects, 187–188
rows (in tables), 110, 260
    adding, 119–120
    coloring, 115–116
    deleting, 124
    resizing, 129
    selecting, 114

rules for form field data entry, setting, 232–233

S

Save As dialog box, 44–45
saving
    field data to databases, 237
    form results, 235–239
    frame pages (framesets), 145–146
    graphics, 82
        formats, 80
    Web pages, 37, 44–45
        format, 35
        within framesets, 146
scanners, inserting graphics from, 85, 166
scheduled images, inserting, 201–202
ScreenTips, 25
scripting push buttons, 229
scroll bars (for frames), 152
search forms, for discussion group users, 214
selecting tables/table elements, 114
selecting text, 51–52
selectors (of CSSs), 66
servers. *See* network servers; Web servers
services, displaying, 7–8
shadows, for objects, 190
shared borders (of frames), 134, 260
    avoiding using, 138
    setting up, 153–154
SharePoint Team Services, publishing importance, 197, 219, 222, 233, 244
Show History command, 24
single page templates, 12
site maps, 203–204
    creating, 208–209
Site Summary reports, 250
Site Usage reports, 250
sizing handles, 182
smart tags, 54, 260
snapping objects to other objects/the grid, 192

sound effects
    background sound, 168–169
    linking to hover buttons, 170–171
spacing frames, 150–151
spacing text, 63, 64–65
special effects
    colors, 159
    Dynamic HTML effects, 176–177
    fill effects, 188
    font effects, 63, 161–163, 164
    for graphics, 89–97
    marquees, 173–175
    multimedia inserts, 160–161, 164–173
spell checking, 70–72
splitting cells, 112, 120, 121
splitting frames, 147–148
squares, drawing, 183
stacking order (of objects), changing, 193
starting FrontPage, 3–4
style sheets. *See* Cascading Style Sheets
styles (line styles), 180, 181
styles (text styles), 66–68, 260
    applying, 66
    creating, 66–68
    modifying, 68
    types, 66
sub-webs, deleting, 248
subheadings, creating, 66
Submit button (on forms), 222, 228
Swap Picture effect, 176, 177

T

table of contents, 203–208, 214
    creating (inserting), 204–208
    display options, 205
    resetting, 205
    types, 203
Table of Contents page, wizard options, 9
table properties
    changing, 127–128
    coloring tables/table elements, 115–116

Table Properties dialog box, 127–128
tables, 109–132, 260
 captions, 122–123, 125
 coloring, 115–116
 converting text to, 118–119
 copying text in, 125
 deleting, 124
 drawing, 111–113
 elements, 110
  See also cells; columns; rows
 entering text, 113–114
 formatting, 116–117
 inserting, 110–111
 inserting graphics in, 125–127
 moving around, 114
 properties. *See* table properties
 selecting, 114
tabs, HTML and, 119
target frames, 134
 editing, 152–153
task panes, 3
 restoring, 4
tasks (Web sites), 24, 252–256
 adding spelling corrections as, 72
 Assigned To reports, 253
 assigning, 252, 254
 completed tasks
  listing, 25
  marking, 255
 creating, 24–25, 254
 displaying assignments, 256
 multitasking, 30, 259
 performing, 255
 review status, 252, 254
 status information, 253, 256
Tasks view, 252, 253
 showing, 11
TCP/IP protocol, 42
template wizards (for Web sites), 5
templates, 2, 260
 color templates, 116
 creating Web sites with, 5–11

 frames page templates, 134
 making accessible, 141
 single page templates, 12
testing hit counters, 198
text, 49–87
 adding to graphics, 90–91
 aligning, 63–64
 animation effects, 162, 176–177
 blinking, 162
 capitalizing, 162
 citation text, 163
 coloring, 157
 converting to tables, 118–119
 copying, 52–56
  in tables, 125
 definition text, 162
 delimited text, 118–119
 entering, 50–51
 finding and replacing, 58–61
 finding the right word, 73
 formatting, 61–63, 161–163
 hidden text, 162
 indenting, 65
 marquees, 173–175
 moving, 52–56
 pasting, 53–54, 56
 selecting, 51–52
 spacing, 63, 64–65
 styles, 66–68
 wrapping
  in cells, 131
  around graphics, 95
text areas (on forms), 218, 222
 inserting, 222–223
text boxes (on forms), 218, 222
 initial values, 224
 inserting, 222–223
 names, 223
 resizing/moving, 107
text hotspots, 105
 adding, 106–107
TGA format, 80

themes, 22–23, 260
    and background color, 156
      formatting Web pages with, 22–24
    and horizontal lines, 69
    selecting, 10
Themes dialog box, 23–24
Thesaurus, 73
threaded replies, for discussion group
    posts, 214
3D objects, 191
thumbnails, 145, 260
    resizing, 88
TIFF format, 80
timed images (scheduled images),
    inserting, 201–202
timestamps, inserting, 202–203
Title bar, 3
toolbar buttons, ScreenTips, 25
Transmission Control Protocol/Internet
    Protocol, 42
transparent color in graphics, 95–96

U

UNC (Universal Naming Convention), 246
Under Construction icon, generating, 9
underlines, adding to text, 61, 162
ungrouping objects, 194
Uniform Resource Locators (URLs), 14, 42,
    246, 260
Universal Naming Convention (UNC), 246
updating Web sites, 247–248
URLs (Uniform Resource Locators), 14, 42,
    246, 260
User Defined Style, 66, 260
user feedback options
    discussion groups, 213–216
    forms, 8–9
user resources, 213, 214

V

validating form field data, 219
verifying hyperlinks, 19–22

video clips
    inserting, 171–172
    linking to hover buttons, 170–171
    play options, 172–173
view tabs, 3
views, 3, 260
Views bar, 3
visitors. *See* user feedback options; user
    resources

W

wash out effect, 93
watermarks, 160, 260
Web
    inserting graphics (pictures) from,
      82–83, 126, 161
    linking Web pages to, 13
Web folder, 18
Web page editor, default, 4
Web pages, 2, 260
    adding, 12–14
      in frames, 138
    background color, 156–159
    background sound, 168–169
    blank pages, 4
    buttons. *See* navigation buttons
    categories. *See* categories (of Web
      pages)
    closing, 32
    comments, 196
    confirmation pages, 214
    content. *See* content
    displaying, 20in HTML format, 34
    editor, 4
    entering text, 50–51
    finding and replacing text, 59–60
    footer options, 9
    formatting
      with style sheets, 66
      with themes, 22–24
      See also special effects
    forms. *See* forms (on Web pages)

header options, 9, 173

hyperlinks. *See* hyperlinks

inline frames, 141–144

linking

to external pages, 40–41

to internal pages, 102–104

linking internal pages to the Web, 13

moving, 16–17

navigating, 32–33

new features, displaying, 7

opening, 14–16

multiple pages, 30–31

previewing, 36–37, 42–43

printing, 42, 43–44

publishing, 246–247

renaming, 12

saving, 37, 44–45

format, 35

within framesets, 146

saving field data to databases, 237

spell checking, 70–71

types, 21–22

Under Construction icon, 9

unlinked, 30

wizard options, 6

writing on, 77

Web servers

names, displaying, 249

publish destinations (locations), 245, 246

publishing requirements, 197, 219, 222, 233, 244

Web settings, checking, 248–249

Web sites (webs), 2, 260

checking, 11

closing, 27–28

components, 195–216

content. *See* content

creating, 5–11

deleting, 248

discussion groups, 213–216

files. *See* files

finding and replacing text, 60–61

managing, 243, 247–256

names, displaying, 249

online surveys, 216

opening, 14–16

pages. *See* Web pages

planning, 2

publishing. *See* publishing Web sites

renaming, 249

reports. *See* reports for Web sites

spell checking, 71–72

tasks. *See* tasks (Web sites)

template wizards, 5

updating, 247–248

user feedback. *See* user feedback options

user resources, 213, 214

webs. *See* Web sites

What's New page, wizard options, 7

Window menu, navigating Web pages, 33

windows, FrontPage window, 3

wizards, 5, 260

Web site template wizards, 5

WMF format, 80

WordArt text, 260

inserting, 74–75

words

finding the right word, 73

selecting, 51

Workflow Status reports, 250

wrapping text

around graphics, 95

in cells, 131

writing on Web pages, 77

Writing Pad, inserting handwritten text, 76–78

X

XML (Extensible Markup Language), 73

applying formatting, 74

vs. HTML, 73

Master Microsoft's Newest Applications with Help from

SYBEX® MASTERING™ BOOKS

ISBN 0-7821-4000-9
1,392 pp • $49.99

ISBN 0-7821-4001-7
752 pp • $39.99

ISBN 0-7821-4003-3
1,200 pp • $49.99
Available 8/01

ISBN 0-7821-4002-5
896 pp • $39.99
Available 8/01

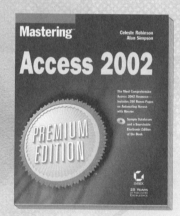

ISBN 0-7821-4008-4
1,224 pp • $49.99

SYBEX®

www.sybex.com